POST–COMMUNIST POLAND:

From Totalitarianism to Democracy?

POST–COMMUNIST POLAND:

From Totalitarianism to Democracy?

Edited by
Jacques Coenen-Huther
and Brunon Synak

NOVA SCIENCE PUBLISHERS, INC.

Art Director: Christopher Concannon
Graphics: Elenor Kallberg and Maria Ester Hawrys
Book Production: Michael Lyons, Roseann Pena,
                Casey Pfalzer, June Martino,
                Tammy Sauter, and Michelle Lalo
Circulation: Irene Kwartiroff, Annette Hellinger,
                and Benjamin Fung

Library of Congress Cataloging-in-Publication Data

ISBN 1-56072-146-4

Post-communist Poland : from totalitarianism to democracy?
   / Jacques Coenen-Huther and Brunon Synak, editors.
      p. cm.
   Includes bibliographical references and index.
   ISBN 1-56072-146-4 : $59.00
   1. Poland--Social conditions--1980- 2. Poland--Politics and
government--1989- 3. Post-communism--Poland.
I. Coenen-Huther, Jacques 1937- II. Synak, Brunon.
HN537. 5.P63 1993   93–28213
943.805'6--dc20   CIP

© *1993 Nova Science Publishers, Inc.*
   6080 Jericho Turnpike, Suite 207
   Commack, New York 11725
   Tele. 516-499-3103 Fax 516-499-3146
   E Mail Novasci1@aol.com

Printed in the United States of America

TABLE OF CONTENTS

Part III – ADVANCES TO A PLURALISTIC SOCIETY

Part IV – MARKET ECONOMY AND SOCIAL SOLIDARITY

Part V – SOCIOLOGY AND SOCIETY IN POLAND TODAY

INTRODUCTION

Jacques Coenen-Huther and Brunon Synak

In the fall of 1989, after the collapse of the Communist regime in Poland, the new government embarked upon a courageous program of economic reforms designed to help bridge the gap between Poland and the developed societies of Western Europe. For the people who after several decades, had this first opportunity to take their fate into their own hands, the goal was altogether ambitious and simple: to return to Europe, to civilization, to "normal life". It was the beginning of the so-called "shock therapy" which was expected to produce results in the short term. And indeed, positive results were rapidly to be observed. However, the transition from a post-totalitarian society to a truly pluralistic one, allowing the free development of a wide range of private initiatives, proved to be much more difficult than previously expected. There was progress, but there were casualties on the road of progress. And rather soon, the process of change seemed to entail serious risks of further social disruption. Decision-makers discovered once more that, no matter how well intentioned reforms are, chains of interdependence are very often the source of unintended consequences.

There was a new need for sociological studies providing insights in the social context of economic and political decision-making. Sociological thinking is very relevant indeed in such circumstances. By placing emphasis on the structural constraints which reduce the margin of freedom of decision-makers, sociological analysis can induce some caution and remind of the very limits of any voluntaristic action. Fortunately, there is a strong sociological tradition in Poland, and this tradition survived fifty years of intellectual regimentation by the two totalitarian regimes of our century. There is also a strong tradition of sociological commitment to the welfare of the Polish people, dating back to the early days of the Polish Republic, after the end of the First World War.

In the Spring of 1992, Polish sociologists from various parts of the country congregated in Gdansk, the birthplace of the Solidarity movement, with the help of some Swiss colleagues, to discuss problems of the post-Communist transition. In this book, the reader will find the major contributions to this seminar.

In the course of the 1980s, growing symptoms of anomie, in the form of alternation between apathy and unmanageable explosions, had been noticed several times. During that period, such anomic tendencies were clearly produced by the deterioration of living conditions, combined with a sense of helplessness: there was a widespread feeling of being unable to influence the course of events, reinforced by a crisis of confidence in the institutions. In the present conditions of transition to a market economy, the necessity of adopting unpopular measures and the need to defer gratifications once again, clearly leads to new forms of anomie. As much as the previous ones, they should be a matter of concern. This is what the two first chapters, by Brunon Synak and Mira Marodi, are alluding to. The specter of the "unfulfilled promises" of which Mira Marody reminds us, still haunts Polish political life.

The previous regime encouraged people to take it for granted that all problems were a matter of State responsibility. At the same time, there was a growing skepticism about the real possibilities to provide solutions. The State apparatus, having proved unable to cope with the problems it had annexed to its area of competence, suffered a serious crisis of legitimacy. Insofar as efficiency became the major criteria of evaluation of governmental performance, this deficit of legitimacy has not yet been reduced, the more so since it was necessary to retain the majority of the cadres of a bankrupt regime. Although, as Jacek Wasilewski puts it in Chapter III, we are clearly witnessing "the beginning of a second restructuring of the political system", and new elites have still to emerge. Uncertainties in this respect are clearly reflected in Kazimierz Frieske's analysis in Chapter IV. On the side of the population, an attitude of grumbling passivity, still expressing itself in terms of "they" and "us" is well spread. To judge by the data presented by Ewa Jurczynska in Chapter V, it becomes urgent to establish the relations between the State and civil society on a new basis. However, fragile but real advances toward a pluralistic society are to be seen in the relations between the "demanding" minorities and the State, as analyzed by Janusz Mucha in Chapter VI. True, ethnic tensions which had been "completely hidden for forty years" have re-emerged with obvious strength. But, as Mucha aptly remarks, neither the demands of cultural minorities nor the reaction of the majority could have been possible "before the democratic transition." In the process of change, the dismantling of a controlled mass media system is certainly a crucial element. Clearly, several decades of totalitarian regimes have left an imprint on mentalities and on attitudes towards the media. But for better and for worse, the change in this field is already far-reaching, as Henrik Galus shows in Chapter VII. Nevertheless, further adaptation to a pluralistic environment remains necessary.

In spite of the massive rejection of a discredited regime, some basic values of socialism are widely shared in the population. They are combined with Christian humanism and other traditional values linked to a sense of belonging to a menaced national entity, to form an original synthesis in which egalitarian feelings, a spirit of solidarity, the right to work, and expectations of social protection play an important role. This value orientation still helps to shape Polish attitudes towards privatization. Janusz Erenc and Krzysztof Wszeborowski contend in Chapter VIII that its importance was probably underestimated by the early promoters of economic reforms. As for individual farmers who managed to save their economic independence throughout the Communist period, they find it hard to adjust to the rules of the market. According to Krzysztof Gorlach and Zygmunt Sarega (Chapter IX), the newly acquired freedom seems to be more menacing in the short term than the previous harassment by local bureaucrats of the former regime.

The three last chapters of the book deal with the relation between sociology and society. Jacques Coenen-Huther (Chapter X) sees the revolutionary changes taking place in central and eastern Europe as a source of inspiration for sociological analysis. Piotr Sztompka (Chapter XI) suggests that the lessons of post-Communist transition might be of wider significance for sociological theories of change in general. Finally, Antoni Sulek (Chapter XII) describes the repercussions of the changes in Polish society on Polish sociology as a discipline and as a profession.

Neither this book nor the seminar of which it is one of the outcomes would have materialized without the financial resources provided by the Polish Sociological Association and the Swiss National Funds for Scientific Research. We gladly acknowledge the support of both institutions. But there was also a problem of language. Although all authors wrote their contributions in English, none of them is a native

English speaker. This is the reason to express gratitude to Martha Baker (Munich) for her invaluable help in editing the manuscript and correcting our language mistakes.

PART I

DIVERSITY OR ANOMIE?

1

THE POLISH SOCIETY: FROM HOMOGENEITY TO DIVERSITY

Brunon Synak
Department of Sociology, University of Gdańsk

M any people, especially foreigners, ask today: What happened to that wonderful Polish society so much admired at the beginning of the 1980s? Why has it, as a renowned sociologist put it, "imperceptibly transformed itself into an unpredictable and self-endangering mass, which is explainable only by the fact of its long subjugation to Communist rule?" (Szacki 1991, p. 10) What happened to the people who respect no decisions of their elected representatives? What happened to the leaders of the opposition who are now fighting one another? What happened to the younger generation who in the past participated in mass pilgrimages to Czestochowa and today march in protest against teaching religion in schools?

I do not propose to offer any ready answered here, but only some suggestions which might contribute to finding answers. My basic assumption is the self-evident claim that, compared to the Polish society of the post-Communist period, the same society during the Communist period was relatively uniform and well-integrated--especially with respect to its basic values, attitudes and ways of behaving. The process of transformation has changed both the extent and the basis of this differentiation. Previously, both the scope and the basis of the differentiation were determined by the attitudes of individuals towards the Communist system and its institutions. Today the differences manifest themselves in many areas in various ways. They reflect the pluralistic character of the newly created system. This is natural and understandable, since the emergence of a modern society has always entailed the processes of fragmentation and disintegration of the social bonds underlying the fundamental solidarity upon which traditional societies were built.[1] I think, however, that the claims about universal uniformity and unanimity of the Polish society in the period of struggle against communism suggest an unnecessarily simplified picture. It is equally difficult to accept the view which seems to be gaining in popularity that chaos and conflicts are immanent and permanent features of the new society. The new ways of reacting and behaving in the Polish society which we are witnessing reflect primarily a change in the adaptive (economic and political) conditions. The explosion of divergent ways of behavior, of diverse attitudes, aspirations and values took place after the main goal had been achieved, that goal which had been the main platform of integration for the majority of society. Freedom has released forces and aspirations which up to then were blocked and covered by the blanket of hatred of the Communist yoke. It seems that this radical transformation has produced a "pendulum effect." New sources of social integration have not yet had time to emerge, while old identity structures--especially Solidarity as a social movement and the Catholic Church as the locus of national values--have lost much of their vitality. This pendulum effect is the source of many contemporary radical and extremist attitudes which are now fostered by practically unlimited possibilities of their articulation and decreasing levels of social control.

1. Constrained homogeneity

The Polish society of the pre- and post-breakthrough period, the period following the Round Table and the parliamentary elections of 1989, has been described in numerous sociological studies (contemporary Polish society is often considered to be the most-studied European society). The majority of those studies are diagnostic and descriptive in character. There is, however, a dearth of theoretical

---

[1] The traditionalism of the Polish society of the Communist period may be called a "forced traditionalism," simce both the shape and the level of people's aspirations was limited by the standards of modern societies, while the means of their supplying were typical of traditional societies (see: Marody 1991).

explanatory models and of medium-range theories (Professor Sztompa's "model of social becoming" is a conspicuous exception in this respect). The diagnoses consider a disease called "the crisis" (Szmatka and Uhl, 1991, p. 361) as the dominant illness of the Polish society of the 1980s. Crisis is taken here to mean both the existence of certain negative phenomena and a progressive transformation of the social system. The Great Transformation, however, both with respect to the form in which it is manifested and its cause has entered a qualitatively new phase of development.

The Polish society of earlier decades was described primarily in terms of social anomie, alienation, deprivation, hopelessness, senselessness, apathy, frustration, etc. Although today one could say that some of these diagnoses were unduly alarmist, collectively they presented a rather good characterization of the society. These phenomena were the result of internal contradictions of the so-called "real socialism." They resulted from an incompatibility of the values and aspirations of Poles--which were derived both from the Christian tradition and socialist ideology--and the limited capacity of the system to deliver. The average Pole had to deal simultaneously with the meager resources at his disposal, a feeling of lack of security, and an insufficient supply of ideals, norms and values (Szafraniec, 1991, p. 198). An extended period of obstruction of restriction of the possibilities of realization of commonly accepted values has led to a progressive deterioration of the normative sphere of the society, to the weakening of social bonds and to social disintegration. Hence many sociologists find social anomie--alienation and deprivation--to be the most conspicuous feature of the Polish society of the 1980s (Kojder 1992; Marody 1987; Synak 1991; Sztompka 1982; Werenstein- Zuławski1991a).

The clash between widely accepted values and the social and political corset of the system prevented their realization and resulted in a peculiar dissonance between the accepted and the implemented principles, between the values of the private and the public spheres. These sphere were mostly the manifestation of contradictory ethos-systems, namely the ethos of national-religious ideology and the ethos of "real socialism." To the public (sacral) sphere belonged the uniform territory of behaviors, attitudes and officially propagated values. The private sphere, on the other hand, was extremely individualized and diverse, although with respect to such basic values as patriotism, religious values, etc., it was relatively homogeneous. The open duality of those spheres reflected a discrepancy between norms of behavior and values.

The axiological dualism was strongly reflected in the structure of the society. A federation of primary groups was a correlative of the private sphere, while the "unfriendly world of institutions" was the correlative of the other sphere. Between the level of primary groups and the nation united by autotelic values there was a "sociological vacuum" caused by the lack of mediating structures and bonds. This axiological and structural duality resulted in a dichotomy: "society vs. state" or "we vs. them." The atomization of the society and the deepening hiatus between the two poles was additionally fostered by the governmental opposition to all forms of spontaneous activity and expression (Staniszkis 1991). Hence the natural tendency of the society to self-organization at the level of microstructures and a withdrawal from participation in public life, as well as abdication of all efforts to effect broader social changes. Thus the "strategies of survival" (Werenstein-Żuławski 1991a) became progressively more common. Such strategies, which became much more pronounced after the introduction of martial law, aimed either at preservation of social values or dealt with economic problems within the so-called "second society."

During this period there emerged parish help-centers for the families of members of Solidarity who were interned, incarcerated, fired or harassed by the authorities. In the name of the values constituting the Solidarity ethos, people would participate in clandestine meetings and organize illegal actions. This was the basis, on the one hand, for a strengthening of communal bonds and mutual help, and a confirmation of alienation from official values and hostility towards state institutions. Such social behavior, internally unifying and homogenizing the society, would appear in periods of peril and would subside with its abatement or with ascendance of the conviction that it was impossible to overcome the threat. Hence it would be extremely risky to claim that the crisis of the Communist system by itself was conducive to profound integrative processes within the society. Much more convincing, on the other hand, seems to be the claim that a clear identification of the goal (i.e., abolishing the Communist system) has created the impression that the regime was facing not individuals but a monolithic collective agent--the Nation or the Society (Szacki 1991, p. 14). This feeling of integration and homogeneity had its source in the moral and axiological character of the protest against the economic and political reality. (The moral values uniting the society and its acknowledged leaders are permanent components of the Polish ethos during nationally difficult periods. (Karolewicz 1992, p. 74).

Soon after the victory of the Polish Revolution, the myth of the society's homogeneity burst like a bubble and the level of its integration proved to be much lower and less sturdy than had been believed. It was characteristic for this revolution that it was not effected by a select group or social class. It was carried out by a wide alliance of diverse social groups which cut across all traditional class, occupational, regional and ethnic boundaries. The avant-garde of the "Polish August" and Solidarity's struggle comprised shipyard workers and miners, engineers and teachers, priests and artists, farmers and intellectuals, students and retirees, Catholics and atheists, Kashubians and Mountaineers. The goal of the bloodless revolution--or evolution, if you wish--was a glue strong enough to invalidate all the differences. The paramount goal was crushing the Communist opponent, and only few wondered what would come after. The unexpectedly easy and quick victory exposed the new face of the social reality. It exposed the illusory character of the assumption that a transformation of the political system will leave untouched the social unanimity, that Solidarity would continue to be the nation-wide social and political movement and that the charisma of its leaders would guarantee "social harmony," that the new economic order would guarantee all citizens relative well-being and better life perspectives. It proved to be an extremely simplified--not to say utopian--vision of the new reality.

2. Eruption of diversity

The overthrow of Communism exposed, on the one hand, the superficiality of the homogeneity of the old society and, on the other hand, accelerated the economic, political, ethnic, and moral diversification of vast social groupings. Democratization resulted in the destruction of the dichotomic social structure (the governing and the governed) imposed by the totalitarian system, and in a diversification of interests among the previously subjugated population. It generated new differences and antagonism. Since this new group diversification is in a state of flux, there appeared in the social consciousness a picture of a society which was extremely complex and volatile. It is still too early to say if there has already emerged a clearly defined structure of interest groups necessary in a market economy and a pluralistic system. This process is to some extent retarded by the old ethos of a society as axiologically homogenous in its resistance to the regime. Nevertheless, the major division of the Polish post-totalitarian society seems to run along the lines of divergent economic interests. The present changes open different possibilities to different groups. The force which drove the society to abolish the old system was the conviction that all, or almost all people would be winners: this turned them into one enormous interest group. The only losers were to be the "perpetrators of evil": the Communist nomenklatura. It is true that the Communists lost their power, but did not lose their access to economic resources and many of them have secured strategic and lucrative posts in the changing economy. The majority, on the other hand, suffers from deepening economic deprivation, and fewer and fewer people feel that freedom and democracy are a sufficient recompense for their material losses. In economic terms it seems justifiable, however, to talk of three sections in society in terms of the possibilities opened to them by the current changes (Werenstein-Żuławski 1991, p. 231).

1. Those who gain by the changes: the new political elites, local authorities and administrations, businessmen, experts, much of the private sector operatives;
2. Those who lose by the changes: the old elites who did not move into business, small farmers, state farm employees, state business employees, small city dwellers;
3. Those who experience no significant changes but who face the prospect of more losses than gains: this part of the society is employed in establishments relatively untouched the transformations, where there is a growing anxiety and fear of the future.

This stratification, which has little to do with a permanent or "class" structure, to a large extent parallels the emotional attitudes toward reality and the levels of acceptance of current economic and political changes. One could say that the results (especially economic) experienced by individuals give rise to their "generalized attitude" towards the whole transformation.

The economic differentiation of the society is a factor which strongly antagonizes and disintegrates the post-Communist society (Giza-Poleszczuk 1991, p. 95). This is due to a prolonged influence of ideology according to which equality was to be the basic element of the projected social order. This ideology contained no rules for differentiating the economic claims of individuals or groups. The only criterion legitimizing one's desire for a better life was the fact of "being a human being" and a member of this society (Marody 1991, p. 234). At present, fulfilling these conditions does not suffice, since market economy has its own "laws of prosperity" (which for many denote the laws of the "unfriendly world of market economy") and which is only very slowly gaining public acceptance. This is why there still exist today strongly emotionally loaded stereotypes of "rich people" (plutocrats), "nouveau riche" and "crooks", while the categories of "businessman" or "entrepreneur" penetrate the social consciousness only with great difficulty. The Polish society would welcome a capitalism "with a human face," that is one without capitalists and pronounced economic differences. This model of social order is quite an abstraction for the majority of the people. It is more a product of "wishful thinking" which conflates "capitalist" rationality of economic relations and freedom of speech with a "socialist" vision of a paternalistic state taking care of its citizens and demanding little involvement on their part (Marody 1991, p. 257). Such thinking seems to result mainly from the very nature of post-totalitarianism, defined as a "socio-economic system which ... gives the impression of being politically and culturally pluralistic, with liberal postulates ... (while), organizationally and socially, it is still a cohesive outcome of the long-standing reign of the authoritarian regime." (Podgórecki 1991, p. 90).

The disintegrative power of the current economic changes in Poland is also a result of the objective fact of marginalization and considerable impoverishment of certain groups, a phenomenon also observed much earlier in Hungary (Szalai 1989). These groups find the transition strongly disadvantageous and they experience it as a kind of declassation. The situation engenders diverse tensions in individuals and in entire social groups, dividing people, instead of bringing them together. Paradoxically, the crisis increased the need for self-help and self-organization, and at the same time breeds tendencies which atomize the society.

It is understandable that the emergence of the Polish political scene should function as a factor strongly differentiating and fragmenting the society. The political antagonist, the Communist Party, disbanded suddenly and rather unexpectedly. On the political stage, only Solidarity and several small political parties "in statu nascendi" remained. This marked the beginning of the process of rapid internal diversification of Solidarity, accompanied by its loss of identity. After the Solidarity victory at the polls in 1989 the new government enjoyed wide popular support but lacked a political base. A social vacuum appeared which had to be filled by various political options of Solidarity lineage. The society forcibly faced an important dilemma which to a large extent remains unresolved to this day. On the one hand there was a pressing need to create political parties derived from Solidarity, and on the other hand, there was a need to preserve the "pristine" image of Solidarity as well as a pronounced antipathy towards political parties in a significant portion of the society. That is why the transition of Solidarity from the "romantic" to the "political" phase (Rychard 1992, p. 24) proved to be so painful. It engendered not only estrangement between veteran freedom fighters who were now creating different parties, but, more importantly, led to a fissure within the nation as a whole.[2]

---

[2] The most significant fissure was created by the "round table" and the presidential elections of 1990, when the two most prominent members of "Solidarity", President Walesa and his chief advisor Mazowiecki faced one another.

The process of populating the political space is perceived by a significant portion of the society as a betrayal of the Solidarity ethos, as a struggle over posts and particular interests. This impression is deepened by frequent changes of governments (there have been three Solidarity government administrations since 1989) and infighting and turmoil in local governments.

The difficulties in creating a civic society result not only from a lack of competence in performing new tasks or from "intractability" of current economic problems. Of great importance is the persistent image of the authorities as a "foreign body." In a totalitarian system this lack of bonds between the state and society was a premeditated feature of the system. State domination and control bred the feeling of alienation and hostility towards the institution and was not conducive to identification and cooperation with the government. Although the present model of the state is based on different premises, the feeling of alienation from various agencies and levels of government persists.

The attitude of hostility towards competing actors in political life and intolerance for political or ideological differences is another example of persistent "Communist residue." A post-totalitarian society would find it much easier to replace the rejected doctrine with another single "total" doctrine that to accept political pluralism. "Thinking in macro-social categories falls to pieces in the era of post-totalitarianism," writes Podgórecki . "However, no political doctrine takes its place automatically. People are unwilling to acknowledge that there is no one synthesizing true philosophy of thought and action." (1991, Podgórecki p. 96).

Thus, a deepening isolation of the authorities and a return to the old division of "authorities vs. society" may in the future become a serious threat to the political stability of Poland. This danger is signaled by the deepening feeling of alienation in the last couple of months. It is visible in the decreasing levels of conviction among the people that they have something to say about what is happening not only in the country but even in their own community.[3] What is more, comparative analyses of the dynamics of contesting consciousness of the Polish society from 1980 to 1990 indicate that symptoms of persistence and tenacity of the conflict situation seem to be much more definite than symptoms of its decline or positive dissipation. This regularity seems to be gaining

---

[3] Opinion polls conducted by the Center of Social Opinion Polling how a significant drop in the people's conviction that they exert any influence on the course of events. While in 1990 11% of the sample claimed that they see a decrease in their influence on the course of events in the country, and 10% said that their influence on how things go in their community has shrunk, in February of 1992 the percentage of such responses was, respectively, 29 and 30.

rather than losing significance.[4] Current conflicts are no longer as polarized as they used to be when monocentric authority was one of the poles of the conflict. Contemporary conflicts are situated on various levels. Hence, the ways the society is divided are much more complex. There has been an increase, for example, in the acuteness of the conflict between city and farm, among political parties, and antagonisms stemming from the support for different leaders in public life. Increasingly, more and more people perceive the political changes taking place in Poland simply as an ."exchange of elites" and not as a radical reconstruction of the system (the perception is strengthened by continual parliamentary quarrels and the instability of the governing coalition). Hence, the majority of the society perceives a rebirth of the division of the influential "them" and the "powerless" us. Hence, furthermore, the structural conflict between the authorities and the society, to a large extent defused in 1989, may be reborn and grow into power. The rebirth of the antagonistic structure is aided by the prolonged economic crisis, [5]especially by the reduced standard of living, unemployment, lowering of the level of expectation of future improvements and the disillusionment resulting from unfulfilled promises of consecutive administrations.

These factors delay the process of creating new social bonds. They entice people to return to their learned hopelessness, increase their sense of deprivation and of the pointlessness of all their efforts and thus contribute to the spread of social anomie,[6]that is, of the phenomena most characteristic for the previous period. At the base of these developments there is a clash between the possibilities, demands and conditions generated by the new economic and political order, and the habits, expectations, and modes of behavior learned in the long process of adaptation of the previous system (see Marody 1991). In a sense, this clash generates deprivation and other negative phenomena at a much deeper level than during the oppressive reign of the totalitarian system. The sudden change of the authorities from "them" to "our people" has led to a sharp increase in expectations (especially economic expectations), while the possibilities of their being met under the conditions of market economy proved to be dramatically smaller than had been expected. What is more, the shrunken possibilities were accompanied by the necessity to change one's attitudes, ways of behavior and values. The transformation of our economic and political order makes social

---

[4]While in 1988 48% of the nationally polled sample believed in existence of social conflicts in Poland, in 1990 they comprised already 61% of the respondents (Jasiewicz 1991).

[5]All opinion studies conducted in the last three years indicate a consistent growth of public dissatisfaction over the conditions of life and the changes in Poland.

[6]It is highly significant that in the last two years in Poland the number of serious crimes and suicides has sharply increased.

consciousness more economy-oriented and favors domination of values relative to the material conditions of life over the values of the higher order, which certainly include the sense of social solidarity. Many values change their placement in the hierarchy while others are replaced by their opposites: e.g., the apotheosis of social equality has been driven out by the glory of getting rich; the orientation toward being "average", by the struggle to prove oneself better than others (Kotlarska-Bobińska 1990). This situation produces a sense of confusion, chaos and anomie.

When we talk about the differentiation within the post-totalitarian Polish society, we must not fail to mention the moral, religious and ethnic aspects of the social changes. In the sphere of morality the process of reinterpreting the norms continues; some even talk of moral (hyperinflation" (Mariański 1991). In a structureless and dynamic society this is the source of transitional, ephemeral opinion groups cemented by a common evaluation of a given norm (e.g. dealing with abortion or the death sentence). This process has recently gained considerably in importance.

The Roman Catholic Church is suffering a serious erosion of its integrative role. Its traditional social and political functions have, to a large extent, been taken over by public institutions and political parties, thus reducing the sphere of its legitimate concern to matters purely religious. Opposition activists who during the period of martial law cooperated closely with the church represent independent political bodies with particular points of view and interests today. Other churches and denominations have gained more freedom for their activities, while among Catholics themselves discrepancies between professed values and beliefs propagated by the Church have clearly emerged (the most significant differences deal with sexual issues; Mariański 1991).

Although the Polish society is relatively homogeneous in ethnic terms, the greater freedom of activity and autonomy of ethnic groups is accompanied by an increase in prejudice and intolerance toward ethnic minorities (for example, toward Germans and Jews). This phenomenon seems to be an immanent feature of transformation in post-totalitarian societies (it is especially acute in Yugoslavia and post-Soviet countries) which pay a high price for the long period of suppression of differences. In this situation, which results from the disarray in the social structure, and in absence of clear social interests of particular groups, one may expect that the basic concept in which the longing for social cohesion can be integrated will prove to be the idea of a nation. It may foster the growth of nationalism as one of the basic components of political orientation (Marody 1991, pp. 266-267).

3. Return to normality?

The noticeable increase in the diversity of the present Polish society results from at least three basic factors: First, the society has for many years lived in an atmosphere of suppressed conflict and apparent uniformity of opinion. The abolition of political barriers favors the activation of many interests which are in open conflict with one another. In other words, the destruction of the political structure of the Communist system has eliminated the basic axiological conflict (the conflict centering on such values as freedom or democracy) which masked the antagonistic interests of individual social groups. The values lying at the basis of the conflict, despite the divergence of group interests, contributed rather to the integration of the society than to its fragmentation (Wnuk-Lipiński 1991). Second, the need to differ in particular areas is not only a natural reaction to the previous situation, but is also a feature of the initial phase of the development of a pluralistic society in which particular groups increase their individual identities by stressing their difference from other groups. These differences pertain to new group interests and to their emergent value systems. Third, there has emerged a significant enlargement of the public sphere (or a "publicization" of the private sphere) and many of the values which used to belong to the private sphere can now be articulated publicly. The truly free and pluralistic mass media are proving to be an especially powerful propagator of these differences (see Lakasiewicz 1991).

Thus, the present phase of the post-totalitarian transformation of the Polish society contains new processes of disintegration, atomization and a reemergence of certain negative phenomena born out of the previous system. The Polish revolution has entered the phase in which illusions about the homogeneity of the society as a whole die and-- as Szacki nicely put it--"the prosaic of everyday living" in an impoverished, tired and fragmented society begins. The consciousness of illusions about an erstwhile homogeneous society should not, however, conceal the fact that many of the present divisions and differences in the society are merely superficial and apparent. It may be expected that after the period of demonstrative diversification a trend toward unification of groups with common interests, a social reintegration and reconstruction of medium-range social bonds, especially at the local level, will emerge. The return of the social pendulum to "normality" or "equilibrium" depends primarily on the question as to when the present transformation will begin to result in positive economic gains for broad social groups.

Bibliography

GIZA-POLESZCZUK S. (1991): "Stosunki międzyludzkie a życie zbiorowe." In: M. Marody (ed.), Co nam zostało z tamtych lat--Społeczeństwo polskie u progu zmiany systemowej. London, Aneks, pp. 69-105.

JASIEWICZ K. (1991): "Od protestu i represji do wolnych wyborów." In: Adamski W. et al. (eds). Polacy '90. Konflikty i zmiana. Warszawa, PAN, pp. 99-122.

KAROLEWICZ J. (1992): "Przywódcy i poczucie bezpieczeństwa w społeczeńtwie." In: Ekspertyzy zespołu doradców socjologicznych OKP. Warszawa, PAN, pp. 73-74.

KOJDER A. (1992): "Mechanizmy korupcji." Warszawa, 59pp. Manuscript.

KOLANKIEWICZ G., P.G. Lewis (1988): "Ponad -- Politics, Economics and Society. "London, Printer Publishers.

KOLARSKA-BOBINSKA L. (1990): "The changing face of civil society in Eastern Europe." Warszawa, PAN. Manuscript.

'LUKASIEWICZ P. (1991): "Porzadek społeczny w potocznych wyobrażeniach i przekazach. "Warszawa, PAN.

MARIANSKI, J. (1991): "Relatywizm moralny w okresie przemian społecznych w Polsce." In: A. Sułek, W. Wienćawski (eds.), Przełom i wzywanie. Warszawa-Toruń, PTS, pp. 224-336.

MARODY M. (1987): "Antynomie społecznej świadomości." Odra, 1, pp. 12-17.

MARODY M. (1991): "Jednostka w systemie realnego socjalizmu." In: M. Marody (ed.), Co nam zostało z tamtych lat -- Społeczeústwo polskie u proju zmiany systemowej. London, Aneks, pp. 220-252.

NOWAK, S. (1984): Społeczeústwo polskie czasu kryzysu w świetle teorii anomii. Komitet Polska 2000, Jabłonna.

PODGÓRECKI A. (1991): "A concise theory of post-totalitarianism (Poland 1989-1990)," The Polish Sociological Bulletin, No. 2/94, pp. 89-100.

RYCHARD A. (1992): "Dylematy rozwoju przestrzeni politycznej," In: Ekspertyzy zespołu doradców socjologicznych OKP, Warszawa, PAN, pp. 23-25.

STANISZKIS J. (1991): "Dylematy lat osiemdziesiątych w Polsce," In: J. Mucha, G. Skąpska, J. Szmatka (eds.), Społeczeństwo polskie u progru przemian. Warszawa-Wrocław-Kraków, Ossolineum, pp. 191-220.

SYNAK B. (1991): "Polish society. Integration and anomie." In: Polnische Hafenstaedte im Umbruch. Universitaet Bremen, Bremen, pp. 49-60.

SZACKI J. (1991): "Marzenia i rzeczywistść polskiej demokracji." Res Publica, No. 5, pp. 10-17.

SZAFRANIEC K. (1991): "Syndrom nienasycenia -- antropologiczne askepty pewnego pokolenia." In: A. Sułek, W. Winclawski (eds.), Przełom i wzywania, Warszawa-Toruń, PTS, pp. 198-209.

SZALAI J. (1989): "Social crisis and the alternatives for reforms." In: A. Toth, L. Bagor (eds.), Hungary under the reform, Budapest, Hungarian Social Sciences, pp. 33-51.

SZMATKA J., I. Uhl (1991): "Polskie społeczeństwo i socjologia -- perspektywy i alternatywy rozwoju." In: J. Mucha, G. Skąpska, J. Szmatka (eds.) Społeczeństwo polskie u progui przemian, Wrocław-Warszawa-Kraków, Ossolineum, pp. 355-371.

SZTOMPKA P. (1992): "Dilemmas of the great transition," Cambridge, Mass., Harvard University, Minda de Ginsburg Center for European Studies. (mimeographed)

SZTOMPKA P. (11982): "Dynamika ruchu odnowy w świetle teorii zachowania zbiorowego," Studia Socjologiczne, No. 3-4, pp. 69-93.

WERENSTEIN- ZUłAWSKI J. (1991a): "Strategia przetrwania i jej koszty." In: J. Mucha, G. Skącpska, J. Szmatka (eds.), Społeczeństwo polskie u progru przemian, WrocLaw-Warszawa-Kraków, Ossolineum, pp. 315-337.

WERENSTEIN- ZŁAWSKI J. (1991b): "Trzy obiegi--trzy kultury. Struktura
społeczna i komunikowanie w dzisiejszej Polsce." In: A. Sułek, W.
Winclawski (eds.), <u>Przełom i wyzwanie</u>, Warszawa-Toruń, PTS, pp. 225-
241.

WNUK-LIPIŃSKI E. (1991): "Derywacje spoŁeczne a konflikty interesów i
wartości." In: <u>Polacy '90. Konflikt i zmiana,</u> Warszawa, PAN, pp. 15-35.

2

STATE AND SOCIETY IN POLAND

Mira Marody
Institute of Sociology, University of Warsaw

The issue on which I would like to focus here is how habitual expectations, attitudes and patterns of action shaped during the years of the Communist regime affect the current developments in Poland. The concepts of state and society play an important role in this analysis, because of the logic of reforms which are now being introduced in this country. These are focused first of all on the transformation of general systemic principles. One of the hidden assumptions is that "capitalist" institutional structures will produce a "capitalist" society. The former are identified with a market economy and a democratic political system, the latter with a competitive society which should emerge as the result of institutional changes.

The new systemic rationality can be summarized in the phrase "as little state involvement as possible." In the economic sphere this means, first of all, the withdrawal of governmental subsidies for plants, enterprises, and agriculture and the privatization of the economy in a later stage. In the social sphere it means giving up the idea of a "protective state." In both cases, a belief in the effectiveness of an "invisible hand" has replaced the former belief in the necessity of statist interventionism. Impersonal political, economic and social mechanisms are meant to take over those functions which, under the Communist regime, were realized through the decisions of the state, or strictly speaking, of those representing its political and administrative authorities. The role of government should be limited, therefore, to the preparation of institutional structures for these mechanisms.

In other words, there is a tendency to think that now that the Communists are out of power and the necessary institutional changes have been introduced, becoming a competitive society depends only on the will of the Polish citizenry. Such an expectation ignores the fact that Communism was not only a specific type of political regime but also a peculiar type of social system which introduced its own institutional structures in all spheres of social life. They have been shaping social practice and social experience for the last forty-five years of Polish history. Habitual ways of coping with social reality which emerged as a result of this experience have been internalized deeply enough to become a natural and obvious mode of being for individuals. In a collision with new systemic rationality they may, therefore, produce results quite different from those assumed by reformers. In this sense, knowledge about the social habits shaped over the years of the Communist system may prove to be of utmost importance in our understanding of current developments.

1. Social habits

The most essential factor forming social practice and its related expectations towards the state was that at the beginning of the post-war period. Polish society was furnished with a system of institutions and principles by which to function which were not a natural result of social processes. Rather, they were designed according to a doctrinaire vision of a "perfect society." The Communist society intended to be the embodiment of all the fundamental ideals of humanity--equality, justice, freedom, abolishment of exploitation, respect for human dignity, and total fulfillment of social needs. The blueprint for such a society was to legitimize the Communist regime, while the party, holding all power in its hands, became the main executor and guardian of the Design. The requirements imposed upon society were, over time, limited to only one: that it should not disturb the work of implementing the Design (Marody 1991b).

Thus, at the foundation of the peculiar political contract binding state and society, a division of roles was laid out according to which the people were meant to profit from the benefits of the system while leaving all the executive decisions to the prerogatives of the authorities representing the state. Narojek (1986) calls this a "nationalization of the initiative of social actions" by which he means that the Communist Party assumed complete, unshared control of social life. Politics, perceived as an exclusive domain of the appropriate authorities, became the main tool for running the society (Marody 1990).

When speaking about the contract I do not mean that the division of roles was accepted willingly on the part of the society. Rather, it was imposed on it be the Communist regime over years of painful social training. The sphere of politics was always most diligently guarded and controlled by the authorities and any attempts of "unauthorized" persons to get into it were most speedily and severely punished. It made politics into a peculiar sacrum). It was, so to speak, a negative sacrum, whose influence radiated upon all spheres of social life, but whose boundaries were rarely crossed, and then only reluctantly and in situations of extreme necessity.

Nevertheless, the expulsion of the society from the sphere of politics was not only achieved by sheer physical coercion. There was also a kind of implicit consensus and tacit agreement binding both sides of the rule-ruled relationship. The terms of agreement contained the promise of a better life to be created by the authorities for the society (Marody 1987).

The results of sociological surveys conducted in Poland in the 1980s clearly show that the complaint of "unfulfilled promises" was the reason most frequently given for lack of obedience to the state powers. In the popular perception, this was the main cause of social disorders, far more important than, for example, frustration with the incompetence and corruption of the administration, or its repressiveness (Marody et al., 1981; Rychard, Szymanderski 1986).

Although the initial division of roles had at its roots a vision of an ideal system, it shaped social practice in quite a real way for forty-five years and let to the emergence of certain beliefs, attitudes and expectations which began to influence people's behavior not only in the sphere of politics but also in other spheres of social life. Three of them seem of particular importance when we try to analyze the present conditions of post-Communist societies.

The first is a set of particular expectations towards the state and the authorities representing it. During the entire period of Communist rule, the state was identified with policies which were above all a source of threat to the average person. It was a direct threat which struck at those who, purposefully or unknowingly, crossed its boundaries. It was also an indirect threat in so far as political decisions by authorities which regulated all manifestations of social life were subordinated to a rationality different from that of the average person and, as such, introduced an element of unpredictability and uncertainty into a social reality to which people had somehow grown accustomed.

On the other hand, politics during this entire period was also a source of hope. A hope for a better life, which would be delivered by the authorities to the society. A hope which was diminishing under the experience of everyday life, but re-emerging with amplified strength every time there was a change of governing personalities. A hope which not only turned politics into the fundamental tool for the distribution of all social goods but also their fundamental source. In this sense, state politics took over the place of economics in social consciousness as the basis of social affluence.

If in the Communist system, politics was an area of sanctity, then peoples attitudes to this sanctum most closely resembled the disposition of the disciples of the cargo cult.[1] In both cases, we are dealing with expectations of gifts from outside the people's world, controlled by powers whose behavior is capricious and fear-instilling. In both cases, there is an emphasis on just distribution and also an identical lack of interest in the processes necessary for the creation of the desired goods or states of social reality. And finally, the basic category on which the behavior within the sanctum is based, in both cases, on categorical faith. A faith in ancestors who are sending ships and planes with cargo or correspondingly, a faith in political leaders promising quick implementation of "normal life."

Secondly, the division into those who are "authorized" to make decision concerning social life and those who do not have such a right has resulted in a re-definition of basic dimensions of the social space in which individuals act. The social vs. the individual distinction predominant in Western societies was replaced with the public vs. the private one in the societies of real socialism.

Many authors have pointed out the crucial importance which the division into "authorities" and the "society", "them" vs. "us", played in the countries of the former Communist bloc. It was perceived as the main dimension of social integration and has promoted the development of negative solidarity, the based for which was a general social interest pitted against the "selfish" interests of those in power. We must remember, however, that this division was far from precise and difficult to make in everyday life. On the one hand, in the system in which every job position was an element of the multidimensional structure of the

---

[1] Cargo cult is a religious movement located in the SW Pacific Islands holding that spirits of ancestors will return and bring with them the large cargoes of modern goods for distributing among its adherents. I borrow this comparison from P. L. Berger (1986) who used it in relation to the role which the modernization ideology played and is still playing in the countries of the Third World.

state, everybody became involved to a greater or lesser degree in the implementation of the Communist design. On the other hand, the rationality of the system was different from the everyday rationality of individuals (Marody 1991b) that people had to find a way to combine both of them. The public vs. private distinction was a solution to the problem.

At first the distinction marked a difference between two spheres of social life: one controlled by the Communist state and the other in which individuals could make their own decisions. As functionaries of the state, citizens were expected to act according to the systemic rationality which was aimed at realization of the design, whereas in their private activity they could have goals different from the ultimate goal of the system. However, with the passage of time, the separation of public and private roles resulted in the emergence of two separate sets of behavioral attitudes, neither of which had much in common with the rationality of the design (Marody 1988).

In general, the attitudes connected with public roles can be described as being governed by the principle of minimalizing one's effort. Because of this different rationality, acting in a public role was perceived as hazardous. The most popular strategy was thus an attempt to avoid responsibility by waiting for the decisions of persons higher up in the official ranks. The "public"-related attitudes had a distinctly defensive character. They were conducive to formulating "negative" goals of activity such as "not to suffer losses," "not to expose oneself to danger," "not to provoke undesirable effects," "not to let others succeed," etc. On the contrary, the "private"-related attitudes had an expansive character and actions were motivated by the hope of success, ambition, curiosity, as well as greed. For "public" attitudes, the most characteristic was the attitude of "learned helplessness" whereas the "private" ones were characterized by the readiness to take risks.

Thus, the division of roles on the "macro" level had as its counterpart the division into "public" and "private" standards which governed the individual activity on the "micro" level. Acting "for the system" became axiologically separated from acting "within the system." The system and whatever acted on its behalf was perceived as alien, "not mine," a source of threat rather than a guarantor of rules which could be used to defend one's rights. A retreat into private life was, in a sense, a natural consequence of such a perception.

Last but not least, the public vs. private distinction which arose from the initial division of roles has changed not only individual behavior but also the patterns according to which it was "socialized." By "socialized" I mean the widespread patterns of individual cooperation or the ways through which common supraindividual goals, rules, and interests are being established among the population. There were two such basic patterns which emerged as a result of the confrontation of human aspiration and needs with the systemic changes introduced by the Communist regime.

The first pattern arose from the adaptation processes. It copied the family matrix as the basic standard for cooperation of individuals on all levels of social reality. Personal ties and personal loyalties became the basis upon which common goals and interests were established. It divided society into small informal groups fighting against each other for access to the resources of the Communist state. It involved "ethical dualism" which allowed individuals to suspend moral norms in contacts with members of out-groups and to consider the claims of such groups as illegitimate and threatening to the well-being of one's own group.

The second pattern of socializing individuals' behavior arose from social protests. It generated the feeling of unity and solidarity in response to threats perceived as external. The society-at-large, very often identified with the nation, became the basic reference group, and the state or rather its leaders, the main enemy. Individuals unified in an effort to dismiss the threat, suspended their everyday goals and ways of behavior. The place of these goals was taken over by a general social interest identified with an ideal vision of "normal life." Social behavior was to be governed by basic norms of human solidarity appealing to moral rather than legal obligations.

The first pattern of socializing transformed the society into an aggregate of primary informal groups, whereas the second pattern resulted in short-term feelings of unity which disintegrated in a collision with the reality of everyday life. Both undermined the existence of the state as an entity subordinating the activity of individuals to the generally observed norms and rules of behavior. The first did so by attempts to "re-privatize" them, the second by trying to replace them with moral norms. Both also eliminated the need for creating new institutions of social life by the individuals. The first did so by directing people's attention to the possibilities of individual and collective "setting up" in the existing institutional order, the second by restricting their political activity to the search for better leaders promising the quick implementation of "normal life."

To summarize the expectations, attitudes and beliefs of Polish society towards the state, it can be said that the "obey or rebel" alternative created the basic pattern of popular reactions developed under the Communist regime. Neither one of these left room for an autonomous functioning of the society; both made social behavior of individuals dependent, directly or indirectly, on the decisions of state.

2. The transition to what?

All of the above-described expectations, attitudes and beliefs became internalized deeply enough to survive the change of political system (Marody 1991a). Their persistence is now additionally reinforced with some structural characteristics of Polish society which make difficult the spontaneous emergence of alternative democratic ways of social behaving.

First of all, the idea of democratic competition presupposes the existence of social groups whose different interests influence the choice between alternative goals and ways of social development. I would like to stress here that the world "social" means that group interests should be a derivative of social structure with the latter reflecting the basic mechanisms of societal differentiation. In the case of post-Communist Poland the problem, however, is that all significant social groups owe their existence to the policies of the former Communist state and do not have any "objective" interests independent of the state, be it Communist or post-Communist (Mokrzycki 1990; Ost 1990). The economic relations of each social group with the rest of the society were and still are mediated by the state and their interests can be defined only vis-a-vis one another. Up to now, even the interests of the emerging group of private businessmen depend mostly on state decisions. It was noticed that private enterprises are flourishing mainly in those areas where state regulations are so imprecise that they allow making money without being engaged in productive activity.

The conflicting character of present social interests in Poland stems from the fact that each group competes with all others for access to social resources distributed by the state and not from competing programs of how to produce these resources, which they could negotiate among themselves. Under such circumstances, the state and, strictly speaking, the authorities representing it, are still perceived as the only group responsible for the goals and means of social development which reinforce the old division into those who take part in making politics and those who do not. (Marody 1991a).

The informal, spontaneous ways of socializing individuals' behavior which were established in the Polish society during the years of coping with a social reality controlled by the Communist regime also seem to be a poor basis for the emergence of groups able to articulate their interests in social terms, i.e. in terms of common characteristics of individuals' social positions. Groups which were formed as the result of adaptation processes were based on personal ties and loyalties rather than on structural characteristics connected with social differentiation of interests. They reflected situational alliances between individuals occupying different social positions and were oriented toward the "re-privatization" of this part of the state's power, regulations, and/or other resources which were controlled by the particular members of a group. In the case of the second pattern of socializing which arose from social protests, the society-at-large became the main group of reference. The interests of individuals became absorbed in general societal interest defined in terms of abstract values.

Both patterns prevent the emergence of groups based on social differentiation of individual interests. The first does so by facilitating the emergence of common interests across the social structure and at the same time by constraining them to local groups, the second by subordinating the individual and group interests to a general societal one. In the first case, group interests are differentiated but cease to be "social," in the second case they are "social" but cease to be differentiated. Both patterns of socializing also promote the definition of individual interests vis-a-vis the state. The first does so by making people sensitive to all the opportunities created by state regulations, which allow a "transfer" of state assets for the individual or group benefit, the second by defining societal interests in opposition to an "unjust" state policy.

The existence of informal ways of socializing individuals' behavior not only prevents the emergence of groups able to articulate their interests within the social structure but also reinforces the division into "public" and "private" sphere of action, with the latter expanding to an enormous degree. What is not controlled by the state--and according to the new rationality almost nothing is--becomes "private" and is regulated by rules and norms specific to the given informal group. This phenomenon strongly affects the chances for the emergence of other characteristics of democratic order.

The prospects for a successful functioning of a democratic society are not only determined by the existence of social groups which are able to define their interests independently of the state. A democratic order requires compliance on the part of all significant interest groups to both the institutional arrangements regulating the negotiation of conflicting interests and the outcomes produced within this regulated competition. As many authors have pointed out, the essential difference between the authoritarian and democratic systems is that the former are characterized by uncertain institutions and certain (at least for strategic groups) outcomes, whereas the latter are based on the certainty of political rules and the uncertainty of political outcomes (Bounce 1990; Bielasiak 1990). Thus, the successful functioning of a democratic system requires, on the one hand, the recognition of formal-legal procedures as the only basis for resolving social conflicts and, on the other hand, the readiness of all significant social groups to engage in give-and-take interactions, the outcomes of which are not known in advance. Both conditions are in opposition to the social habits shaped in Polish society over the past 45 years of Communist rule.

There is still a strong belief that the state and the authorities representing it have sufficient power to change any institutional decision that opposes a commonsense understanding of justice and that use of this power depends only upon good will. Moreover, in the Polish society, the popular understanding of justice is strongly connected with an orientation towards "consensus and interpersonal harmony," whereas an orientation towards "law and order" does not play any significant role in shaping this social construct (Jasinska-Kania, 1988). One can expect, therefore, that even with established institutional arrangements (the conditions for which have not yet been created in Poland), formal decisions unfavorable to strategic groups may result in social protest. Of course, social protests take place in Western democracies, too; what makes them particularly important in the Polish case is that they are perceived here as the only feasible form of popular participation in policy-making and the "final" argument in situations of social conflict.

Chances for the recognition of the uncertainty of institutional outcomes as a natural element of democratic competition also seem rather law, taking into account the established social habits. First of all, the "natural" social strategy under the Communist regime was "take-and-keep" rather than "give-and-take." The defensive character of public-oriented attitudes resulted in perceiving others as rivals and not partners in bargaining processes. The orientation to the certainty of institutional outcomes was also facilitated by the development of the Solidarity movement, in both its legal and illegal phases. One should remember that the unity of Polish society in the 1980s was, after all, based on the premise that the "society as a whole" deserves a better or "normal" life. This has been further reinforced by the rhetoric of post-Communist political elites who have appealed and still do appeal to popular consensus and to moral rather than interest-based aspirations. It is not surprising, therefore, that the growing financial differentiation of the population is now perceived more as a betrayal of Solidarity ideals than as a natural consequence of economic mechanisms triggered by institutional reform. It means, however, that the chances for the recognition of uncertainty of outcomes as a natural characteristic of economic political processes are still very low, whereas the chances for social protests are constantly increasing.

To sum up this line of argumentation, I would like to say that although Poles are competing all the time and in all spheres of social life, they can hardly be described as a democratic competitive society.

Both their patterns of socializing individual behavior as well as habitual expectations, attitudes and beliefs make them competitors for a share of the pie being distributed by the state. Disintegrated, fixed on its expectations and interests as shaped by the former statist system, and living with the dream of a strong leader who would resolve all the problems accumulated over the years of Communist and post-Communist experiments, Polish society might seem well prepared for an authoritarian dictatorship.

In any case, the temptation of an authoritarian solution is quite strong for the new political elite. At least some of its leaders, seeing themselves confronted on the one hand with social demands which cannot be satisfied because of the desperate condition of post-Communist economy and, on the other, with the necessity to fight for survival against other parties in the political arena, would see in some authoritarian measures the way to discipline both society and their own political rivals.

However, the same social habits which are now postponing the transition to a liberal democracy also cause the chances for the introduction of an authoritarian model to be rather small. None of the political parties is able to mobilize the support of a significant social group which would allow it to take over and to keep the state power for a longer period of time. With the Communist economy already collapsed and market economy not yet established, they can offer their potential supporters only some hope for the future and some substitute satisfactions for the vast economic and psychological hardships. And it is not enough for people who are longing for actual solutions of their present concrete problems.

We can expect, therefore, a continuation of the present political situation which resembles neither a democratic nor an authoritarian model. It is strongly conditioned by a state policy which is being shaped by two opposing tendencies. The first arises from a dogmatic attitude towards liberal economic principles adopted by the present political elites. It is based on the belief that the state should not influence processes of social self-organization and that society itself is able to generate such institutions which it needs. The second tendency arises from the habitual expectations of society towards the state. It takes the form of constant social demands, the basis for which is the belief that nobody but the state is responsible for the well-being of its citizens. Both partners of the state-society relation ascribe to each other competencies and possibilities which do not actually exist.

Nevertheless, the first tendency relieves the government from the necessity to outline any programs for social reconstruction; the second forces it to satisfy the demands of at least some groups. In practice, state funds are being intercepted by those whose protests might be more dangerous for the systemic stability and those with higher institutional competency instead of being used as the tool for structural reconstruction. Thus, the attempt to reconcile a liberal doctrine with political necessities leads, paradoxically, to reinforcing those people's habits which have developed under the conditions of quite contrary systemic rationality.

The process of systemic transformation aimed at establishing a liberal democratic order which was started in Poland in June 1989 is, in my opinion, irreversible. It does not mean, however, that it is simple, easy, and dependent only on institutional changes. The functioning of society as a _system_ is, after all, a complex result of individuals' everyday activity, aimed not so much at creating a new social order as a "decent" life for themselves and their families. Since this activity is strongly influenced by habitual expectations, dispositions, and perceptions that are regarded as obvious and natural and are, therefore, out of individuals' control, it may produce social results quite different from those assumed by the reformers. Being aware of such a possibility is the necessary (although still not sufficient) condition for being able to prevent it.

Bibliography

BERGER, Peter L. (1986): "Trzeci świat jako idea religijna," Pismo Literacko-Artystyczne, No. 6-7.

BIELASIAK, Jack (1990): "The dilemma of political interests in post-Communist transition." Paper for the IREX-PAN Conference on Socialism and Change: the Polish Perspective. Princeton, October 22-24.

BOUNCE, Valerie (1990): "The struggle for liberal democracy in Eastern Europe," World Policy Journal, 7:3.

JASINSKA-KANIA, Aleksandra (1988): Osobowość, orientacje marolne i postawy polityczne. Warszawa:IS UW.

MARODY, Mira, Jan KOLBOWSKI, Cecylia ŁABANOWSKA, Krzysztof NOWAK, Anna TYSZKIEWICZ (1981): Polacy 1980. Warszawa: IS UW.

MARODY, Mira (1987): "Social stability and the concept of collective sense." In: J. Koralewicz, I. Białecki, M. Watson (eds.), Crisis and Transition. Polish Society in the 1980s. Berg Publishers.

MARODY, Mira (1988): "Antinomies of collective subconsciousness," Social Research, 55: 1-2.

MARODY, Mira (1990): "Perception of politics in Polish society," Social Research, 57:2.

MARODY, Mira (1991a): "From social idea to real world." In: K. Poznanski (ed.), Constructing Capitalism. Westview Press.

MOKRZYCKI, Edmund (1990): "The heritage of real socialism, group interests, and the search for a new utopia," Paper for the IREX-PAN Conference on Socialism and Change: Polish Perspectives. Princeton, October 22-24.

NAROJEK, Winicjusz (1986): Perspektywy pluralzmu w upństwowionym społeczeństwie. Warsaw (Unpublished manuscript)

OST, David (1990): "Interests and politics in post-Communist society: Problems in the transition in East Europe." Paper for the 1990 Annual Meeting of the APSA, San Francisco.

RYCHARD Andrzej, SZYMANDERSKI, Jacek (1986): "Kryzys w perspektywie legitymizacji," in W. Adamski, A. Rychard (eds.), Polacy '84. Dynamika konfliktu i konsensusu. Warszaw, IFiS PAN.

PART II

POWER AND LEGITAMACY

3

TOWARDS NEW POLITICAL ELITES IN POLAND?

Jacek Wasilewski
Institute of Sociology, Jagiellonian University, Cracow

Immediately after the collapse of the Communist system in Poland, in the second half of 1989 and first half of 1990, the political elite which had emerged via Solidarity enjoyed a very considerable autonomy, much greater than is the case of elites in stable democracies. This was due to at least two causes.

First, the new elite gained ostentatious public support. The unambiguous way in which Poles had declared themselves against the old regime manifested itself nation-wide in the election of candidates from the opposition. In a dichotomous political system ("we" versus "them") it could not have been otherwise. The rejection of one option meant the choice of the other. In the elections held in June 1989 the Solidarity elite, as the guarantor of the rejection of the unacceptable system, received from the populace its carte blanche. The public support it enjoyed was particularly strong since it appeared to be a monolith. The new elite entered the political arena as the representative of a mass social movement, and not as an internally structured political force. The electoral program of Solidarity was couched in very general terms. It was based on the rejection of the Communist regime and carried slogans calling for democratic and pro-market reforms. It emphasized the elements of community and blurred the divergencies between the interests of the various groups. Hence, it consolidated the belief that the consensus on the system which was to be rejected was tantamount to the consensus on the traits of the system which was to replace the old. The masses, integrated around that program and mobilized by the electoral success, were all the more ready to submit themselves to the leadership of the elite as the elite included people with various genealogies and leaders who manifested a unity of opinion and a determination of action.

Secondly, the exceptional autonomy of the Solidarity political elite at that time was due to a lack of rivals and the weakness of other structures which usually restrict the actions of elites. The Communist elite disintegrated unexpectedly quickly and ceased to be the principal actor on the political stage, while those oppositional groups which had not participated in the Round Table talks were temporarily pushed to the margin of political life. Moreover, such institutions as business and the army, which under normal conditions exert a strong influence upon political elites, were at that moment--when their political patron disappeared--incapable of acting independently. The Catholic Church was the only institution which could restrict the autonomy of the new elite. It probably did perform that role to some extent, but since the actions of the political elite were essentially convergent with the interests of the Church at that time, the restrictive role of the latter did not manifest itself visibly.

Such a situation did not last long. A social movement, monolithic in the face of the enemy, when it unexpectedly seizes power, undergoes diversification. It becomes divided politically, and hence it split as a movement.

The post-Communist groups also underwent a signal evolution. After the shock of the elections defeat in June 1989 and the self-dissolution of the Polish United Workers Party in January 1990, they gradually reintegrated their followers both through political reinstitutionalization (formation of the Social Democracy of the Republic of Poland as a political party) and the continued "rule of souls" among their still quite numerous supporters. That was to become manifest during the presidential elections in the autumn of 1990 and the parliamentary elections in the autumn of 1991.

Another important process which started at that time was the institutionalization within the political system of those groups which either did not want or could not take part in the Round Table. Their role was growing as a result of the intensifying divisions within Solidarity and the consolidation of the forces on the left and manifested itself in full force in 1991.

The beginning of a second restructuring of the political system thus began within a very short period of time. While the first, symbolized by the Round Table and the dichotomy "we" versus "they," allowed one to speak about the post-Communist political stage, the second, symbolized by "the war at the top," makes one speak also about the post-Solidarity stage.

The three parallel processes which co-determined one another-- the disintegration of Solidarity, the consolidation of the post-Communist left, and the systemic institutionalization of groups which are at the same time non-Communist and non-Solidarity--were the political substratum of that period. All those processes manifested themselves, though in varying strength, in the Parliament, essentially determining the behavior of individual deputies, the Parliamentary clubs, and the Diet as a whole as well.

I shall now try, be referring to the various models of political elites and the empirical data describing the deputies which served in the Diet during the legislative period 1989-91, to shed some light upon the development of the political elite in Poland.

The deputies which served in that contract-based Diet[1] represented various factions of the political elite. Their actions, convictions and mutual relations, as manifested in interviews, provide data which could hardly be overestimated in the study of the elite-making process. The contract-based Diet was one of the few places in which representatives of the majority of the political forces not only met regularly but also nolens volens compared their standpoints and sought solutions. It naturally became the forum for processes important to the formation of the new elite, and especially those which could initiate alliances or coalitions of elites. Accordingly, it is probably the best focal point for researchers interested in the crystallization of the political elite in post-Communist, and soon post-Solidarity Poland.

At the same time, one must realize the limitation of our data. The answer to the question about the shape of the emerging political elite cannot be given on the strength of an analysis of a single political institution which, while very important, is still very specific as well. Every parliament, by the very logic of its functioning, is conducive to the working out of a platform of common actions, formation of coalitions, and the negotiation of political compromises. Witnessing clashes--

---

[1] The Diet was labeled so because it was agreed at the Round Table conference that the Polish United Workers Party and its allies would have 65 per cent of the seats, whereas the opposition groups taken together would receive 35 per cent of all seats. The election to the Senate was to be free.

sometimes in very acute and even "non-parliamentary" forms--of opposing options, but nevertheless reaching agreements, and searching for solutions acceptable to the majority--these are immanent features of every parliament.

1. Political elites and their typology

In contemporary studies of elites (cf. Field, Higley 1980; Burton, Higley 1987b; Wasilewski 1989) preference is given to the positional (institutional) definition of political elites. Such an elite usually includes persons who hold high posts in political institutions and in the largest and most influential organizations of other types (economic, military, trade-unionist, etc.), which affect the exercise of power. For such an interpretation of "elite," consciousness is not taken into consideration. it is irrelevant whether the persons treated as members of an elite treat themselves as such or whether they are treated as such by others.

An elite is not identified as a group of persons marked by special characteristics which make them predisposed to lead the masses. Nor is it a mafia which manipulates will-less masses to satisfy its own interests. It is not, either, as the Marxists used to claim, a will-less instrument in the hands of the ruling classes. In the contemporary elitist interpretation, a political elite is treated as a specific (in view of the consequences of its actions) but otherwise "normal" occupational group, whose members occupy formally defined posts and perform the roles assigned to those posts.

The elites perform an active and independent role in social processes, but in their actions they are restricted by the masses. To put it as briefly as possible, the world-view, the political attitudes, and the decisions made by an elite, and also the relations among its factions and segments, essentially determine the political process and its results. The determinant role of the elite is not fully reducible to other factors: it cannot be reduced to class, ethnic or economic variables. This is not to say that these variables are not at work. On the contrary, they exercise a very essential influence, and their significance manifests itself in the political, economic, and social tendencies dominant in the masses. These tendencies cannot be ignored by the elites because they exist on the condition of having won the support of the masses. Elites always require the support of the masses. It means that their autonomy is confined to a certain area beyond which they cannot move on pain of losing power or the chances of winning.

The members of a given elite try, on the one hand, to win the support of the masses, and on the other, to modify or even create their beliefs. The masses, in turn, try to force the elite to make political decisions which are the most advantageous to their interests. That very intricate and dynamic system functions as long as there is an essential agreement between the convictions dominant in the masses and the policy of the elite. When the divergence between the two passes a critical point the elite is no longer capable of securing the indispensable minimum of support, the system decomposes and the old elite is replaced by a new one. Thus political stability is largely dependent on the essential agreement between the normative systems of elites and the masses.

Most scholars interested in the structure of elites agree on the point that essentially we are dealing with three types (models) of political elites. These types are assigned various names and the factors stressed in their descriptions are distributed in various ways, but if we disregard the details we obtain a surprisingly similar picture.

Type one is an elite which is "totalitarian," "monocratic," "unanimous," or "ideologically unified." The basic characteristic of such an elite (which assumes various forms, sometimes widely different from one another--its model representatives being the Nazi and the Stalinist elites) includes the external appearances of full cohesion, guaranteed by the profession of only one ideology and by the membership of practically all of the elite in one and the same party or movement. Representatives of rival ideologies and political groups are eliminated (by diverse methods), and the system of internal and interpersonal relations within a given elite is fully centralized. The connection between such an ideologically unified elite and a definite political system is very clear. That undemocratic system, whether totalitarian or quasi-totalitarian is, however, marked by considerable stability.

Type two is an elite which is "divided," "disintegrated," or "disunified." Its various factions are fully separated from one another and engaged in a life-and-death struggle. They observe the principle or "all or nothing" and try to eliminate the opponent from the political life for good. The victory of one party (often by extra-legal means, such as a coup d'etat usually results in persecutions of the other party and in a change of the entire political configuration. Divided elites are connected by regimes marked by a lack of both political stability and democracy.

Type three is an elite which is "pluralistic" or "consensually united." It is marked by consensus about the fundamental values, treated as unavoidable, and attachment to a common "political code," which determines the rules of the political game and political succession. The political opponent is a recognized rival (and not an enemy) who is to be defeated but not destroyed. Conflicts among factions are solved by negotiations and not by violence, in accordance with the principle of "something for something." Rival groups communicate with one another, interpersonal relations cut across the boundaries of political groups, and elements of cooperation are nothing exception. Consensually united elites are connected with regimes marked by both stability and democracy.

This simplified typology of political elites includes a clear evaluative element. The desirable type is that of consensually united (pluralistic) elites, because only that type is connected with a stable democratic system. Note, however, that connection between the type of a political elite and the type of political system is not defined unambiguously. It is certainly not a causal nexus. It is rather correlational in character. We are unable to say what the sequence of events is. Is it so that a given system emerges first, followed by an elite of a given type? Or conversely, is the elite "earlier" and the system "later?" It seems likely that both processes are parallel to one other, but even this opinion is debatable. The enigmatic formulation that a given type of political elite "is connected" with definite characteristics of the political system is thus a result of an unsatisfactory state of knowledge.

If the pluralistic (consensually united) elites are the most desirable type in view of their connections with stable democracies, then the key problem is: how are such elites formed? Is it possible, and how, to stimulate their emergence in former Communist countries?

2. Elite settlement--the path toward pluralistic elites

M.G. Burton and J. Higley (1987a) point out several historically developed ways in which pluralistic (consensually united) elites emerge. We shall be interested here only in what they call "elite settlement," the only way which offers opportunities for a quick development of a political elite.

What historical circumstances induce divided elites to seek a settlement? Burton and Higley see two typical situations. One of them is a prolonged and exhausting conflict which does not yield the expected results for those who are parties to it: none of the factions involved in that conflict attains its goals, all of them are losers rather than winners. The realization of that political deadlock induces the parties to seek a compromise and ultimately a settlement which would become the foundation of a pluralistic elite.

The other situation is that of a deep and widely spread crisis which threatens to annihilate the system itself and hence also the divided elites. Such crises are often caused by unexpected change of policy by autocratic rulers, military defeats, or sudden economic collapses. The struggling factions sometimes respond to such dangers with a compromise and the search for a common strategy of opposing the mortal danger, which in turn gives rise to a permanent settlement.

The known cases of settlements reached among elites were marked by several common features, which may be treated as essential accompanying factors. One of them is a legal text in the form of a constitution, a pact, or a political contract, which regulates the obligations of two or more parties and defines the relations among them. Another is the role of the leaders, outstanding and recognized personalities in public life, whose prestige, authority and influence are capable of making the participants in the political game adhere to the legal text in question. The role of experienced politicians proved to be of key importance in both the construction of the settlement and its later implementation. The role of the new leaders in such processes is limited.

The obvious thing to do is to pose the question about the model of the political elite which is emerging in Poland, and especially about the conditions of, and prospects for, the development in Poland of a consensually united elite.

The answer to this question will inevitable require an analysis of many controversial theoretical issues, and often taking a stance in purely political matters. For considerations of space, I am not in a position to go into detail. Furthermore, the empirical data at my disposal pertains to a single and very specific segment of the Polish political elite. Therefore, what I intend to do here, to take a small step toward the full answer to the question formulated above, reduces to a sociological comment on the trends in the evolution of the new elite, an analysis of the chances of an agreement among elites, and the presentation of opinions of deputies on intra-parliamentary relations.

When watching the emergence of the new political elite in Poland, one cannot exclude any of the three models mentioned above as possible outcomes. I am interested above all in the set of conditions which would yield a pluralistic elite, but shall point out arguments in favor of the emergence of an elite via one of the other models.

The evolution of the political situation in Poland in recent months provides numerous arguments for those who claim that we are dealing with the emergence of a political elite which resembles the model of a divided elite. Many things indicate that political groups prefer to entrench themselves in their positions and deepen the moats separating them from their opponents rather than seek a rapprochement and platform of cooperation. The most important in that respect is the deep split within Solidarity, which as resulted in a practical annihilation of that political phenomenon which Solidarity was throughout the 1980s. This was followed by the regaining of lost territory by the post-Communist forces and the growth of the political significance of extreme and populist groups, including those which advocate an alternative development to the model "Europe, democracy, market economy." Essential in this context are also the divisions over the model of the State, means of privatization, the public role of the Catholic Church and its clergy, the agrarian policy and many other issues.

On the other hand, the possibility cannot be excluded that the phenomena we witness will lead towards the emergence of an elite resembling the model of an ideologically unified one within in an authoritarian system. I do not mean the Communist ideology in the form observable until recently. That is part of an irreversible past, which is not to say that the leftist options and leaders originating from the Communist movement will not gain in influence. I mean the ideologization of the Polish political stage over denominations, national and so-called independence-oriented issues. The Polish party system, still unstable and fragmented but already clearly outlined, makes one consider the following possibility: many parties are thoroughly ideologically-minded, often inspired by the sense of their mission and determined to strive toward the implementation of their "only correct" programs.

Both tendencies--one leading to a divided elite or one leading to an ideologically unified one--are supported by the mood of the masses, irritated by the permanent economic crisis and the inefficiency of the new elites.

In Poland, there are, of course, conditions for the emergence of a consensually united elite. Its birth could, theoretically speaking, take place in any of the three ways specified by Burton and Higley. One can exclude neither the post-colonial way (if dependence upon the Communist empire is interpreted as a variation of neocolonialism) nor a gradual rapprochement of opposing political groups accompanying an improvement of the economic situation, nor, a fortiori, a settlement achieved among the elites.

The first situation, described as the post-colonial way, seemed until recently to describe the Polish political stage. The various political forces, shaped in a peaceful and legal struggle, gave the impression of being permanently held together by their common values. They succeeded in institutionalizing their activity (Solidarity) which encompassed an ever wider sphere of problems going well beyond the sphere of pure politics. In the face of the enemy, they formed a monolith held together by convictions which, presumably, were commonly shared. Such a picture of forces opposing the neocolonialists and their local agents spread throughout the society and won its unquestionable support. But it turned out that the consensually united opposition was unable to transform into a consensually united governing elite; once it seized power its pluralistic binding agent broke down visibly.

The second way, the longest and most strongly conditioned by the economic factor and found in most West European countries is, of course, possible for Poland, too. It assumes a gradual evolution of the systems of beliefs dominant in the masses towards a preference for efficiency and anti-egalitarian values. That implies a growing support for political forces building their identity on the basis of those values. The beginnings of that course are visible in the Polish economic policy. But it undergoes periodic breakdowns, does not bring societally tangible effects, and the masses are no longer inclined to accept long periods of privations. They expect quick and effective solutions and make the new political elites responsible for the lack thereof.

The elite settlement, the third way of forming a pluralistic elite, could be such a quick solution. While the second way was based on the assumption that actions of the masses would be the principal determinants of change, in the third way that role is assigned primarily to the behavior of the elites.

Polish society expected effective action on the part of the coherent elite that had emerged from Solidarity. It saw in that elite the main factor which conditioned a systemic transformation. That was why "the war at the top" and the electoral campaigns (presidential in 1990 and parliamentary in 1991), which brutally disclosed a lack of unity in the elite, gave rise to so many unfavorable opinions. The results of the elections were striking and attendance at the polls was low.

The ideal of elite settlement, as seen in the Polish context, must be discussed in greater detail because it gives rise to numerous misunderstandings.

In current views, an agreement among elites is often associated with manipulations carried out by a narrow group of leaders over the heads of the people. Such a procedure is well-known in Poland. For 45 years people experiences such mafia-like agreements among the elites. The fronts of national unity and national revival were arbitrarily formed, alliances were concluded, political parties were merged, coalitions were formed, eternal friendships were declared. That was all being done, of course, "in accordance with the historical interest of the Polish people," or at least of their "leading class" or "progressive majority."

To impart such meaning to elite settlement has nothing in common with the contemporary elitist theories. It is otherwise a pertinent empirical generalization about political practice in undemocratic systems, and by all means deserves a more penetrating historical and sociological analysis. But at this point I want to speak about phenomena which are rooted in the population and the social system, and have been introduced by that population (and not by non-representative elites) into the political system.

In this connection, the question suggests itself whether the contract concluded at the Round Table conference was an elite settlement in the sense established by Burton and Higley. The answer is far from simple.

On the one hand, the socio-economic situation in 1988-89 and the then existing configuration of political forces meet the preliminary conditions outlined by Burton and Higley. There was a deep-reaching crisis, relative equilibrium of forces, political deadlock with no prospect of being overcome within the existing structures, combined with the simultaneous threat to the existence of no only the model of social order but society itself. On the other hand, before the negotiation of the contract and at the time of its conclusion, one of the parties maintained its privileged position in the power structure owing to the circumstances dictated by external factors (The Yalta geopolitical system) and the still obedient apparatus of coercion. But by then that party had practically no support from the masses. It engaged in the negotiations not in order to lay the foundation for a future cooperation with its opponents, but to gain time and save what it could.

It must be said that Solidarity, too, did not engage in the negotiations with the intention of reaching a consensus. It wanted to snatch from the communists what could be snatched in the existing situation in order to drive them in the future from the position they still held. Thus neither party to the contract was intent on laying the foundations of a political system based on division of power and joint government. For the Communist elite, the signing of the contract proved to be signing the death sentence for itself. Does it make sense to speak of a settlement if only one signatory is left alive?

Elite settlement was not the Polish strategy in the struggle against the Communist system. Instead, Poland used the Hungarian strategy which led to a "negotiated revolution" (cf. Bruszt 1990, Kennedy 1990). As I see it, elite settlement in the sense given by Burton Higley is a chance to organize a new political system based on a pluralistic consensus in post-Communist Poland. In spite of external similarities, it was not a way of forming a quasi-pluralistic elite at the time when Communism was declining in Poland.

The strategy of elite settlement cannot succeed against the will of the masses. This is not to say, however that the elites have to wait passively for the development of the dominant options in the masses. In seeking a solution, they can and should influence the masses, formulate new solutions, modify standpoints and programs, and submit proposals.

The duty of the political elites is to be elite, to seek new ways, to make proposals and to anticipate the masses. They should not, however, move too far ahead of the latter, because they then risk being misunderstood and blamed for "elitism," and the price for that would be the loss of support and, sooner or later, of power.

Elite settlement seems to be a possible way whereby the genuine Polish political elites might seek a common platform for actions. "Genuine" means having emerged from the masses, making reference to values articulated by the people, and representing given groups of the population. Can the leaders of the parties and groups active on Poland's political stage be considered such genuine elites? On the whole they are, as evidenced by the results of the elections in 1990 and 1991. And did the deputies to the Diet in 1989-91 form such a genuine elite? The answer to this question is less unambiguous.

On the one hand, the 1989-91 Diet was labelled contract-based just because its structure was not the result of the freely voiced will of the electorate, but was predetermined at the Round Table. It had been known already before the elections that certain political forces would be absent from the Diet, that others would be over-represented and still others under-represented. But, on the other hand, as it turned out later, the elected deputies showed a much broader spectrum of political attitudes than might have been anticipated during and immediately after the electoral campaign. It must be remembered that the configuration of political parties in 1989 was still very weakly developed and did not reflect the real political differentiation. Furthermore, the unprecedented task undertaken by the Solidarity Civic Committees made people manifest their inner unity. And finally, under the specific conditions of Polish transformation, the relations between party authorities and their representatives in the Diet were as a rule ambiguous and unstable, but in all cases complicated. Many a time, deputies manifested political preferences quite different from those they had declared prior to the elections. On many occasions they changed their political affiliations during the term of office by becoming representatives of parties which had not even existed at the time of the elections. The reverse also occurred: parties which succeeded in having their candidates elected were later dissolved. In all, the contract-based Diet, in spite of the stigma of original sin committed at its conception, proved more representative than expected.

That contract-based Diet was practically the only place in which--at the time of our study--representatives of the various parts of the political elite would meet and the essence of the parliamentary system consists in the search for political compromises. In that sense, the data obtained from the deputies may even out the differences among political groups, especially if they were analyzed at the level of political parties, which are naturally more oriented toward the logic of uncompromising struggle.

If it turns out that in the contract-based Diet we find no symptoms of elite settlement, this will mean that the chances of its occurrence in other institutions of the political system are even less, since such institutions are, as a rule, less oriented toward the search for compromises. If, on the contrary, it turns out that symptoms of elite settlement are observable in the Diet, then--paradoxically enough--the prognostic value of such a finding will be relatively limited in view of the specific characteristics of the 1989-91 Diet. Nevertheless the effects of actions of members of that provisional political body may have long-term consequences for the structuring of the entire political stage in Poland, and the model of relations among factions worked out by them may prove to be the binding pattern for future parliamentarians. That is way it is worthwhile to study the deputies of the contract-based Diet.

3. In search of consensus

In every community which remains in systematic spatial contact, group-making bonds develop. It was not otherwise in the case of the deputies to the contract-based Diet. At first, it was a community divided into two camps on a percentage basis of 35% to 65%. As a whole, the deputies formed a body which rigorously observed the division originating from the electoral campaign, divisions which covered not only the sphere of formal roles but also extended to informal relations. In some cases that assumed the form of a specific social ostracism. For instance, deputies from the Solidarity civic committee reported that it had been unthinkable to share tables in the Diet's restaurant with deputies of the left.

But that did not last long. Naturally and inevitably, new bonds started developing, not necessarily along the lines of political and party lines. Joint work in parliamentary committees, living in the same parliamentary hotel, occupational and background similarities proved strong cohesive factors. The deputies, in spite of essential and even deepening political divisions, were becoming a social group.

Reactions to outside dangers were another group-forming factor which consolidated the Diet as a whole. For instance, in their statements the deputies showed unambiguous solidarity in rejecting the idea of photographs or films being permitted in the Diet due to the fact that during plenary debates many seats remain unoccupied. They perceived this as an unjustified attack on the Diet and its method of working. Quite often they accused the mass media of trying to discredit the Diet.

Paradoxically, the Senate was another widely perceived threat to the identity of the Diet. One of our respondents described it picturesquely:

"Now I must say that one can often see something strange and even mysterious. There are moments in which the Diet seems to be integrated, namely when we have to reject an amendment proposed by the Senate... In such cases, we very easily find the two-thirds majority which is required to reject the amendment." (16 PKLD)[2]

It is self-evident that the sense of group bonds which developed among the majority of deputies regardless of their political affiliations is not any indicator of a consensus. But it is an essential platform of social interactions, free from officialdom and the necessity of representing the party line. It allows the development of good feelings and understanding and the emergence of the sense of non-contradiction and even convergence of tasks. It is exactly that element which is stressed by the authors who proposed the concept of elite settlement: exchange of information, mutual contacts, mutual declarations of measures to be taken--in short, conversing with one another.

The issue of the area of consensus which might serve as the basis for the formation of a pluralistic elite of course goes beyond group-making processes. In its main stratum, it pertains to an agreement on the fundamental values, including fundamental political values. Has such an agreement manifested itself in the case of the deputies to the contract-based Diet?

It is not difficult to answer this question. The majority of our respondents declared their attachment to those values which are the key words of the systemic transformation throughout post-Communist Europe:

"On that point all of us are in agreement--both the former opposition and the former party members--that we have to defend democratization, and that the return to the market economy is inevitable." (07 OKP)

"There is agreement on economic matters and the systemic change in the national economy." (20 OKP)

Moreover, some deputies add to the list of those values which, as one of them put it, are self-evidently accepted as common to all of them, such items as "reason of State," "national frontiers," and "national identity."

Declarations of common values on such a level of generality do not authorize one to draw far-reaching conclusions. When one examines

---

[2]While quoting deputies, the number of respondent and his/her club affiliation is put in parentheses. Clubs' abbreviations are as follow: PKLD - Parliamentary Club of Democratic Left (ex-communist party deputies); OKP - Solidarity deputies; PSL - Peasant Party (satellite party); SD - Democratic Party (satellite party).

the statements of the respondents more intensively, one can find essential differences in the meanings assigned to the same terms. That is why the indicators of the area of consensus prevailing in the Diet must be sought not at the level of values treated as slogans, but through the analysis of the full contexts of the statements made by the deputies.

The overwhelming majority of the respondents replied affirmatively to the question whether there matters in the Diet on which there is essential agreement among the deputies. Only two or three stated outright that there was no such consensus. Among those who perceive a consensus in the Diet, one can single out several perspectives.

The first perspective from which consensus in the Diet is perceived is that of voting. It seems that this is the relatively weakest interpretation of consensus, being based on the purely numerical results of voting. There is a consensus because many bills are passed by an immense majority of votes and some of them almost unanimously. This reasoning is represented by relatively few deputies.

The second perspective resembles the first in the sense that it also reflects a weak consensus. Some deputies declared openly that they are aware of the superficiality of the consensus, thereby expressing their doubts as to whether such a superficial or enforced consensus can serve as a basis for political actions.

"There is an agreement at such moments when the cabinet stakes all its authority, which involves a "to be or not to be" for the cabinet ... The opposition also votes for the bills to let the cabinet continue its work.... The opposition realizes that for the present there is no other cabinet capable of maintaining peace and order. That peace and order is the price paid for the consensus on most important matters." (05 PKLD)

"They were not common values; they were problems resulting from definite political configurations... But it was not a consensus based on values, whether moral or ideological. It was based on a certain political configuration." (15 PKLD)

The third type of thinking about consensus stresses the general agreement on economic matters and the general disagreement on political matters. According to this reasoning, acts pertaining to economic matters are based on hard economic arguments. They are discussed in the form of a clash of arguments and the compromise is reached in matter-of-fact debates. On the contrary, political issues are burdened with emotions and demagogy: there is no place for rational arguments, it is a place for invectives, insinuation and quarrels.

The fourth type consists of statements which voice strong convictions that there is consensus in the Diet; it is claimed for all or at lease many fundamental matters:

"This Diet is a positive phenomenon. It forms a whole in spite of all the differences of political genealogies, in spite of the painful differences of the historical past, and in spite of all obstinacies and anger. It is a striking whole which is in agreement about what is most important." (24 PKLD)

"I think that an ever better picture is emerging just now... Negotiations between groups and individual deputies, between the various orientation, are better and better; they are more and more reasonable, balanced and responsible. People do not see things tendentiously. It is not the case that just because I was a member, say, of the opposition or the nomenclature, I must stick to a different view all the time... I think that the psychological sphere, that of the exchange of opinions and human contacts is very important." (12 PSL)

The four types of interpretations of consensus in the Diet described here encompass all comments of the deputies. There are, of course, single cases of other interpretations (e.g., that there is consensus on political matters but none on economic ones), but such statements are not significant as they lack broader contextual substantiations.

When looking at the statements made by deputies in the light of political divisions, especially the two opposing groups, we have to note that representatives of the old regime stress the elements of consensus somewhat more strongly and, on the whole, give the Diet a better assessment, while emphasizing less strongly manifestations of disagreement.

Not all the respondents were convinced that there was a parliamentary platform of consensus, but all of them thought that there were spheres of disagreement. Thus, they agree that there is much disagreement. There spheres of the latter are usually associated with the sphere of ideology and politics, and less frequently with that of economics.

Generally speaking, deputies from the various groups point out different aspects of conflicts in the Diet and stress differently the matters on which opinions differ the greatest.

Issues connected with the past--its assessment and the overcoming of its legacy--are the most strongly accentuated elements of discord. People of the left speak more frequently about the past, but those of the right and from other groups also refer to that subject. Of course, deputies whose political genealogy goes back to the opposition speak about the past mainly in connection with settling accounts with the nomenklatura.

"The first point of disagreement is...settling of accounts with the former authorities. Practically speaking, we have done nothing in that respect. No one has been condemned, no one has been scrutinized, no one has been proven incompetent or dishonest. And yet it is common knowledge that in that period such things were very frequent... I see that the left, whose past has been underscored with a 'thick line', instead of showing compunction... is preparing itself for a new attack, uniting and mobilizing its forces... The entire assets of the former Polish United Worker's party has disappeared. Why? By whose agency?" (26 OKP)

Former members of the Communist Party and its allied parties see that problem quite differently:

"Of course the past (is the subject of discord - J.W.). The past. Too much is stressed by certain groups of deputies." (01 PKLD)

"The main issue of discord is that the 65% part of the Diet ... cannot reconcile itself to the fact that what had been worked out at the Round Table has so quickly lost its validity." (19 PKLD)

"I must say at this point that there is essential discord over the assessment of the past 45 years. The left, of course, does admit that many errors had been committed during that period. But it cannot accept a total denial of everything. That is practically the basic conflict of opinions. We do not abstain from a critical assessment of the past, but we demand an honest assessment, which should take place a little later. We think that it is still too early for such an assessment." (32 PKLD)

The comparison of these statements visualizes the diametrically different visions of the past. What for some is a trifling matter, is for others a problem of fundamental importance; what for some is too early, is for others too late; what for some is a well-deserved punishment for theft, is for others revenge. The conflict over the past arouses strong emotions. The deputies with a political genealogy going back to Solidarity accuse their opponents of cynicism and insolence, whereas the latter complain that they are being exposed to malicious attacks, churlishness, aggression and ill will.

The range of discord in the Diet is vast, but it is only in connection with the past that the dichotomy "we" versus "them" is revived so glaringly. An essential division, but much less intense and not always along the 65%-35% line can be observed on two other burning issues: abortion and Church-related questions (e.g., teaching of religion in the schools, the lay nature of the State, the political role of the clergy). That lower intensity manifests itself in the fact that the standpoints of the opposing groups are usually more balanced and not always clearly contradictory. We also noted on both sides an embarrassment sui generis caused by the fact that problems which should be intimate and personal were brought to the public forum of the Diet.

The next manifestation of a lack of consensus among the deputies is related to the agrarian policy. Here the principal division line separates the deputies from the peasantry who are gathered mainly in the Polish Peasant Party but also present in other groups, from the rest of the Diet. The core of the controversy is the economic strategy vis-a-vis agriculture. Peasant deputies demand the preservation of the existing agrarian structure, restrictions on the import of food stuffs, preferential credits, and purchases of agricultural produce by the state as a kind of State interventionism. The opponents point out that such a strategy would be at variance with the market economy and would petrify the obsolete structure of Polish agriculture and its inefficient modes of production.

Controversies over agriculture are serious and there is little chance of agreement. The Polish Peasant Party is probably the only group in the contract-based Diet which had a markedly class character. Its deputies openly state that they represent peasant interest, and non-contradiction with the interests of the small farmers is the basic criterion of their assessment of all issues, whether political or economic. Such a standpoint usually does not meet with understanding by other deputies who perceive their role differently. In the opinion of the latter, the principal task of the contract-based Diet was to work out the legal foundations of the new political and economic system. Thus, while the peasant deputies wanted to represent the interests of one class only, the remaining deputies treated their parliamentary duties as a historical mission of on the national scale.

Another issue on which there was disagreement in the Diet was the package of bills related to privatization. At issue was not privatization as a macro-economic strategy--a point of consensus--but the ways to implement it. In particular, reprivatization and the protection of the present users of the property were controversial. This issue was raised in principle by deputies of the left when voicing their reservations about the radical ways of implementing this strategy.

4. In search of cooperation

Political scientists are familiar with cases in which political groupings differ very basically in their opinions, with each having a very narrow scope of beliefs, but nonetheless show a willingness to seek common elements and to mitigate discrepancies. Were we dealing with this situation in the contract-based Diet? We asked our respondents about the parties, parliamentary groups, factions, etc., with which they would be ready to establish relations, reach compromises and cooperate in some form, as well as with which even elementary cooperation seemed impossible to them.

Most respondents answered that question in two parts. First, they declared their willingness to establish contacts, to communicate and to seek a common platform with all groups in the Diet. This was then followed by reservations, usually at the personal level. Typical answers were as follows:

"It would be difficult to find a group or party which totally negates the necessity of change, which would solely resort to demagogic slogans and whose presence in the Diet would be an utter misunderstanding. There are no significant groups of this kind in the Diet." (07 OKP)

"For me there are no persons with whom cooperation would be impossible. Otherwise I would see different degrees and spheres of possible or impossible cooperation. My assumption is that in every group, as in individuals, one can find a positive element." (34 OKP)

"I have the soul of a politician and I think that one has to engage in a discussion with everyone." (24 PKLD)

"I see certain group of people from the former Polish United Workers Party who are doing a good job in this Diet. Unfortunately, there is also a large group of those who continue to do destructive work." (33 OKP)

"I think that one can cooperate with everyone. If they are wise people, then I do not classify deputies according to the group they are members of, but according to whether they are clever or average." (04 SD)

The statements quoted above illustrate the dominant conciliatory tune. They voiced at least preliminary readiness to engage in cooperation. Characteristically enough, the greater inclination to accept compromises and to engage in a dialogue was declared by deputies from the "old coalition." It is hard to say unambiguously in the light of the available data to what extent this was a result of a genuine openness to cooperate with Solidarity deputies, and to what extent it was intended to counteract their marginalization in the Diet. One can only suppose that tactics did play an essential role. That would be understandable considering the greater political experience and the standard political principle of taking the side of the stronger party. And who was stronger in the Diet in 1989-91 could be doubted only at the very beginning of that term, when politics was identified with arithmetic, i.e. when 65 was arguably more than 35.

While the majority of the deputies declared their readiness to cooperate with representatives of other factions, we also had a group who were more radical in their opinions:

"I would rather have no contacts with the Marxist-Leninist group, as I call those on the left. I am convinced that they still represent the legacy of the structures formerly imposed upon us. And the Peasant Party also included many people from the nomenklatura, who have, so to speak, repainted themselves and adopted a new name. But there are people there from the earlier structure." (22 OKP)

"I cannot imagine working jointly with the radical wings of the Polish Peasant Party or the Central Alliance, nor with persons who are most strongly associated with the former Polish United Workers Party." (03 OKP)

"Certainly not with the left." (26 OKP)

"I do not much like the formulas which I hear among colleagues who now form various Christian orientations, nor do I like the nationalist options." (19 PKLD)

On the one hand, there were "the obsessed anti-Communists" in the Diet, as they were called by their opponents, and on the other hand, the hard left, nicknamed "the concrete." But in the opinion of the vast majority of deputies they did not play any decisive role, although they were usually noisy and hence could be easily identified.

In the opinions of the deputies on their potential or actual political allies or their opponents no clear-cut or institutionalized divisions predominated. Of course, representatives of the various groups more frequently pointed to politically and ideologically closer groups as their political allies, and more frequently rejected the possibility of cooperation with groups more distant in that dimension, but it was not a clear network of mutual preferences and rejections. It seems important that there was a universally declared willingness to seek compromises and a common platform, or at least to maintain contacts and to engage in a dialogue. That was certainly quite a lot in view of the political genealogies of the deputies and the first period of the contract-based Diet, when it seemed absolutely incapable of performing its function of transforming the country.

5. Polish prospects for a pluralistic elite

At the beginning of the study on the deputies elected in quasi-democratic elections we realized that, on the one hand, they had a historic role to play as gravediggers of the Communist system and, on the other, the institution which they represented was a temporary political entity, created ad hoc, with questionable legitimacy. That split--the epoch-making mission and the provisionality and lack of rooting in the population--was also fully clear to the deputies. But the prevailing attitude was that regardless of the origin and status of this Diet, and regardless of how it would be assessed in the future, the task was to use its prerogatives to the most and to make the unprecedented evolutionary change of the system in Poland work as smoothly as possible.

If one were to look at the prospects for the emergence in Poland of a consensually united political elite solely in the light of the interviews carried out with deputies in the late 1990, one would have few reasons for optimism.

The areas of discord were unquestionably vast, but there were also areas of consensus. Important was that these areas were quite clearly separated from one another. Discord dominated the sphere which Edelman (1964) called symbolic politics and covers the great issues of ideas and morals. Under the Polish conditions, symbolic politics manifested itself above all with reference to the past and its assessment. Consensus was manifested in regard to the policy of the distribution of goods, which primarily determines production and distribution.

Another ground for some optimism could be found in the analysis of statements made by deputies concerning the cumulation of "concord" and "discord" in the various political groups. We did not find any strong polarization of opinions or attitudes in one particular group. There were certainly differences in that respect, but they were not dramatically significant.

The grounds for cautious optimism, as based on the statements of the deputies concerning the chances of a pluralistic elite emerging, had to be revised in the light of the developments in the political situation which took place after we gathered our empirical data. At the time of our study it was still reasonable to suppose that the role of symbolic politics would decline after the turning point of 1989-90, and that for both "objective" reasons (more and more issues related to the past would be solved) and "subjective" (increasing pragmatism). Yet nothing of the kind occurred. On the contrary, ideological and symbolic issues dominated the political process even more strongly. They must have been indispensable for the full self-definition of the participants, thus contributing to a greater transparency of the entire political configuration.

The hypothesis that a consensually united elite emerges through elite settlement makes the assumption that in the period preceding such a settlement the political structure is already full developed. All the actors on the political stage are present, all of them know their own roles and the lines of the other players. All of them have many opportunities to check their own possibilities and those of their partners, all of them try repeatedly to dominate the entire stage by pushing the other actors behind the scenes or slamming doors on the young turks who try to storm the actor's entrance. But all those efforts had proven of no avail. None of the actors who count lets himself be eliminated from the performance. In the long run, such a situation not only prevents a given play being stages but threatens the existence of the theater as a whole. Sometimes, in exceptional situations, the dramatis personae decide to cut the Gordian knot by accepting an interpretation of the text common to all and by selecting a new cast.

This metaphor obviously is out of place in the case of the Polish political stage, mainly because of the lack of a developed political configuration. Such a situation is typical during a systemic transformation when none of the participants in the political process are clearly defined, nor their respective strength fully known, nor stable rules for their mutual relations given (cf. O'Donnell, Schmitter 1986; Linz, 1990). Two well-known students of the transition from authoritarianism to democracy have concluded, in the light of the experience in South America and in Southern Europe, that the transformation processes are dominated by the struggle for the definition of the modus operandi of the political process. This applies very well to the atmosphere of transformation in Poland:

"What we refer to as *transition* is the interval between one political regime and another. (...) Transitions are delimited, on the one side, by launching of the process of dissolution of an authoritarian regime and, on the other, by the installation of some form of democracy, the return to some form of authoritarian rule, or the emergence of a revolutionary alternative. It is characteristic of the transition that during it, the rules of the political game are not defined. Not only are they in constant flux, but they are usually arduously contested; actors struggle not just to satisfy their immediate interests and/or the interests of those whom they purport to represent, but also to define rules and procedures whose configuration will determine likely winners and losers in the future." (O'Donnell, Schmitter 1986: 6)

An elite settlement, and hence the emergence of a pluralistic elite, may take place if the actors firmly occupying the political stage see for themselves that all other solutions bring no results. An elite settlement cannot be based on a "theoretical" diagnosis of the situation or even the most rational arguments pointing out the necessity of a consensus.

The case of Poland seems to confirm the hypothesis advanced by Burton and Higley that the path to a pluralistic elite leads through a divided elite. The processes we have observed in the contract-based Diet and the entire political system from 1990 on, were not only processes in the construction of a pluralistic elite, but, on the contrary, meant the disintegration of an apparent political consensus. One can only hope that this is an inevitable but short stage on the path to the formation of a genuine structure of political forces, and hence a consensual unification of elites. In that sense, paradoxically enough, the quicker the decomposition, and the more painful and profound it is, the better the prospects for a durable political integration.

Bibliography

BRUSZT, L. (1990): "1989: The Negotiated Revolution of Hungary." Paper presented at the Conference on the Role of Party/State Apparatus in Peaceful Transition from Dictatorship to Democracy, Budapest.

BURTON, M.G. and J. HIGLEY (1987a): "Elite Settlements," American Sociological Review, 52, pp. 295-307.

BURTON, M.G. and J. HIGLEY (1987b): "Invitation to Elite Theory." In: G. W. Domhoff and T.R. Dye (eds.), Power Elites and Organizations. Newbury Park: Sage, pp. 219-238.

EDELMAN, M. (1964): The Symbolic Uses of Politics. Urbana: University of Illinois Press.

FIELD, G.L. and J. HIGLEY (1980): Elitism. London: Routledge & Kegan Paul.

KENNEDY, M.D. (1990): "The Intelligentsia in the Constitution of Civil Societies and Post-Communist Regimes in Hungary and Poland." Paper presented at the IV World Congress for Soviet and East European Studies. Harrogate, England.

LINZ, J. (1990): "Transitions to Democracy," The Washington Quarterly, Summer, pp. 143-164.

O'DONNELL, G. and P.C. SCHMITTER (1986): Transitions from Authoritarian Rule. Tentative Conclusions about Uncertain Democracies. Baltimore: The Johns Hopkins University Press.

WASILEWSKI, J. (1989): "Elityzm redivivus?" (Elitism Revived?), Studia Socjologiczne, No. 3, pp. 79-107.

4

BUREAUCRATIC ELITES IN POST-TOTALITARIAN TRANSITION

Kazimierz W. Frieske
Institute of Sociology, Warsaw University

At the end of January 1992 the Chancellery of the President asked some 120 Polish intellectuals, prominent journalists, university professors and celebrities three questions concerning the major challenges and dangers becoming apparent during the social change occurring in the country, as well as about ways to cope with them. Being asked to edit and summarize the answers, I was struck by the constructive disillusionment emerging from those replies. Disillusionment because the establishment of the new social order reveals itself to involve much more difficult and painful tasks than previously expected and promised during the "mobilization" phase of the Solidarity social movement. Constructive because the experience gained within the last 30 months is considered to be crucial for the future and, above all, the way to avoid further mistakes.

What counts now, however, is a diagnosis of the current situation as seen by the Polish intellectuals, among them many social scientists. They focused their attention on the two main areas considered as crucial for the future: the economic system and the institutional structure of society. Leaving aside the economic system, as the subject of an ongoing ideological debate, the institutional structure is perceived to be collapsing. In short, it is seen to be seriously weakened by the process of change, society is becoming more and more amorphous or anomic and, what is perhaps most significant, the State itself is seen as the main source of social disorganization. Critical comments focus mainly on the legal system and its inefficiencies as well as the chaos within the State's administrative apparatus. The latter is seen as riddled with political conflicts and unable to perform its basic function, which is to execute the decisions made at the political level. Based on this diagnosis, there is a call for a "strong government," by which is meant a government of professional, a-political, competent, rational and career-oriented bureaucrats.

Unfortunately, I am afraid, this 80-year-old Weberian dream will remain a dream more than ever under the present conditions in Poland. In contrast to this dream, reality suggests quite different developments which are more or less consistent with the general changes in the functions of political governments in other countries. At the most general level, the very essence of the problem we are faced with now is well-known: the choice between bureaucracy and democracy. Knowledge of both theory and reality of bureaucracy lead me to believe that this is, at least partially, a false dilemma. I consider it false because the real issue of democracy is not "rule by the people," but what institutional controls are imposed on ruling elites and what mechanisms are employed for the recruitment of elites. Nonetheless, some fundamental misunderstandings concerning the meaning of "democracy" still surface in the ongoing discussion concerning political legitimization of the ruling elites, whereby little attention is paid to the old Mosca statement that elites "have themselves elected", or in the debate between those who fear technocracy and those who praise mediocrity. What is at stake in this debate is significant not so much as an interesting puzzle of political theory as involving real life efforts to stabilize political order. And there is little doubt that it needs stabilization. What makes the problem interesting, however, is the intellectual challenges concerning possible forms of such stabilization.

It is convenient and justifiable to start with some popular, commonly held beliefs, for they form the reality faced by every politician seeking public support. From the very beginning of the post-Communist transition in Poland, namely from the first Round Table Agreements and the election in the second half of 1989, bureaucrats who were running the public affairs of post-war Poland were considered incompetent, self-serving, perks-seeking "nomenklatura", appointed mainly for their political loyalty to the Communist Party. As such they were held responsible for the past inefficiencies of the Communist state and considered a major obstacle in the process of "progressive" or "democratic" reforms due to their vested interests in the old political structures. Even the rhetoric of the first non-Communist Prime Minister of post-war Poland, Tadeusz Mazowiecki, who introduced the idea of a "thick line" discriminating the future and the past did not help much. Gradually, due to political pressure as well as the alleged or real incompetence and inability to find a new role in the emerging social order, these people retired from the social and political arena.

This process of bureaucratic elite transformation calls for several remarks. The first is that popular wisdom does not necessarily agree with knowledge gained from more or less systematic and disciplined insight into reality. The findings of a study I conducted at the end of 1987 concerning the careers and intellectual orientations of the bureaucratic elite led me to believe that it was much less homogenous than could be supposed on the basis of commonly-held stereotypes. The principal differences between the professional careers of the people who reached top positions in the central administration were connected with the ways they entered the service and with the dynamics of successive promotions. Some of those who were directors in 1987 had entered bureaucratic hierarchies at the very beginning of their professional biographies, had held successive positions longer than others and are promoted to the level of director relatively quickly. With others, crossing the threshold of the ministry was, to a greater or lesser extent, delayed and they came to the ministry from industry or local governments. The latter often shifted from one employment to another, occupied more positions and held each of them for a shorter period of time.

True, at a certain stage in this climb up the ministerial establishment one had to prove his or her ideological loyalty and join the Communist Party. However, nothing substantiates the idea that the ways of reaching the top were contingent upon this decision. Two other indices of involvement and ideological loyalty, namely the performance of party functions and full-time employment in the party apparatus did not differentiate people. There were some slight differences, but they showed no statistical significance. Again, it is true, that among several types of bureaucratic careers I found one specific, resembling to a large extent the common image of the <u>nomenklatura</u> member. These people frequently shifted from one job to another, often jumping over several levels of hierarchy and holding positions with side benefits, such as in the foreign service, international organizations or trade and industry agencies abroad. They were also, more often than others, at some point during their professional lives, full-time employees of the party machinery. Nevertheless, these directors constituted the smallest fraction of the bureaucratic elite and did not exceed 10% of the sample under study. Obviously, it was enough to provide some grounds for the stereotype of a high-ranking "nomenklatura" bureaucrat but, at the same time, small enough to make its pertinence questionable.

Credit may be given to the succeeding governments and their personnel policy for resisting the temptation of witch-hunting that was called for from numerous corners of the political arena. In plain fact, however, most members of the old Communist bureaucratic elite left the service speedily due to the threat of purges hanging in the air. Thinking in terms of social engineering, I consider this reticence a political mistake, since the most fundamental wisdom of "The Prince" has been ignored. As Machiavelli advised, punishments should incapacitate enemies for light punishments only invigorate the need for revenge. In other words, the "civilized" way of dismissing the people who in bulk were incorrectly labelled as "enemies" of the new social order has only embittered them and led them to an integration in the form of a "dirty togetherness" in order to advance their own particular interests. The fact that society is suffering from corruption and an uncontrolled flow of money, as some economists claim, as well as from informal influences of the former establishment, happens to be a self-fulfilling prophecy. It is true that such conclusions somehow resemble cheap journalism but, on the other hand, I do not think the dynamics of the process allow for more mature theorizing.

As we know, two major roles in the political arena are distinctively separate in terms of the sources of their legitimization. For bureaucrats, status is ascribed according to the position in the organizational order, and for politicians according to public support. It is also well-known, however, that this Weberian distinction is highly inadequate and misleading, at least as far as contemporary political is concerned. Strictly speaking, the impersonal bureaucrat or "technician of power" exists only as a theoretical, abstract construct and no civil servant ever gained any influence without political support. There is little doubt about the plain fact of real life: candidates for crucial positions in every bureaucratic hierarchy are at best nominated for only minimal political considerations, and at worst for purely political reasons. It is also well-known that over time every central administration becomes overgrown with a network of semi-governmental agencies serving as an important complement to the complex political structure. Some of these agencies shelter members of the political opposition, some others are used as informal extensions of the government since they can be useful ways to evade public control over gray areas of political activity or as a way to pay political debts.

In summary, in modern political systems bureaucracy is hardly non-political, and with the growing professionalization of politicians, politics is highly bureaucratic. But, what is interesting and deserves careful investigation is the variety of these phenomena. It is my contention that political bureaucratization or bureaucratic politicalization will be shaped by factors specific to local political traditions as well as the particular traits of a given political system.

From several cross-cultural studies undertaken in the late 1970s and 1980s, we have learned beyond any doubt that in some countries, such as France, Italy, Japan, or--to a certain extent--the USA, political impact on governmental bureaucracy results in large-scale changes among high-level administrators both in centralized and local bureaucracy. In Great Britain and in Germany, central bureaucracies inhibit more and more people who hardly could be labelled career bureaucrats. For example, as early as 1964 Harold Wilson introduced into the Civil Service hierarchies a number of people appointed as political experts, advisors, consultants, etc. Following him, Edward Heath appointed "political secretaries" to serve in advisory capacity to the members of his government. Edward Heath also created an agency called the Central Policy Review Staff which was inhabited quite clearly by political nominees. The same practice has been followed fervently, to an even greater extent, by the succeeding conservative governments. In Germany nobody takes an interest in the fact that high-ranking bureaucrats are also active members of various political groups or the fact that numerous seats in the Bundestag are occupied by ex-bureaucrats. From the time of Willy Brandt's socialist-liberal coalition, numerous experts with clear ties to one or the other political party are on the public payroll, to nobody's astonishment.

Weberian dichotomy should then be enriched and, in fact, be presented as a trichotomy, where the third, missing element is a functional hybrid, namely the people belonging both to the world of politics and the world of bureaucracy. They are the most important holders of power in contemporary political systems. Due to their ability to shift themselves rapidly from the one world into the other, they have access to the heart of power. They are the core of every political system, at one time visible as representatives of the people, at another time, movers of political puppets. In a study of the parliamentary records from 1991 I completed quite recently, it was found that the ways legislators have been using professional knowledge clearly indicate that, first, real work is usually done at the level of parliamentary subcommittees rather than at the level of committees with the latter merely presenting an opportunity for political show. And, second, meetings of subcommittees are infrequently attended by legislators who, when in attendance, are dominated by professional bureaucrats. True, legislators are in a position to accept or reject every legislative proposal, at least in theory, but usually, as long as the given legislation is not politically "hot" they prefer to let the bureaucrats run the show, for they are unable to participate in the professional discourse and have very little to gain in terms of political visibility. There is also another factor which explains this political passivity of the people's representatives. In fact, many bureaucrats are not perceived by legislators as such, but mainly as former colleagues from the glorious times of the fight against the Communist regime, who for a time have stepped into the shoes of a bureaucrat.

It is my impression, at the moment founded only on a careful watching of the political arena, that in Poland (and perhaps in other post-Communist countries as well), the fusion of politics and bureaucracy is even more clearly visible and faster than in other, more stable political system. The logic of my reasoning is as follows:

First, no matter what is said about the so-called "thick line" that is supposed to discriminate between the Communist past and the democratic future, a gradual reconstruction of the bureaucratic elite, for both technical and socio-psychological reasons, has to involve criteria of political and ideological loyalty.

Second, economic instability and the lack of structural embeddedness as well as unstable divisions of the electorate forces members of the newly created political establishment to secure their income with a somewhat modest, but regular flow of money and government perks coming with the positions in the central administration or its agencies.

Third, underdeveloped economic structures and relatively weak links between politics and economy hardly make possible shifts between political elite and corporate elite, so only the positions with the bureaucracy remain as rewards for political service.

Fourth, immaturity is the only recently created political groups still make them unable to support professional party activists, ideologues and think-tank members.

Quite unexpectedly, then, there are certain inconvenient traits of the idol called "democracy" which are more evident when it is observed in the making than when they are blurred by political routines habitually but mistakenly called "democratic." Such disillusionments seem to be naive and trivial for the student of modern political systems. The issue at stake is now whether they are not too great to be coped with by a society that just a short time ago was led by an idol to overthrow the Communist rule.

PART III

ADVANCES TO A
PLURALISTIC SOCIETY

5

CHANGING CULTURAL PATTERNS IN POLISH SOCIETY

Ewa Jurcyznska
Institute of Educational Theory, Silesian University

T his paper deals with the public opinion, beliefs and preferences found in the current political, economic and social transformation from Communism to capitalism (market economy) and a democratic political system. These can be viewed as problematic for the changing patterns of political culture during this systemic transformation.

The meaning of political culture used in this paper is based on the concept developed by G. Almond and S. Verba in their classic work "The Civic Culture." They defined political culture as a set of political orientations toward the political system held by citizens in a given country, its constituencies (institutions), the political parties and their programs, elite and leaders, the elected representatives and mandated officials at the various levels of government. Political culture can be analyzed in terms of the entire society as well as its particular constituencies (classes, socio-professional groups, local communities, particular groups with specific affiliations). An analysis of political culture can focus on the universal features of a given set of political orientations or to the relation between social structure and particular orientations; or to the mechanisms of forming and changing these orientations and relations; and, last but not least, it can refer to the consequences of changes in the patterns of political culture for the entire society and the position of different social groups in social life (in all dimensions).

The problem I would like to present and discuss here relates to the following questions: whether democracy is developing in this first stage of the "Great Transformation" from Communism to capitalism in Poland today; which type of democracy is involved in both the theoretical and practical sense; whether we can observe the formation of an open and democratic mentality or, on the contrary, the continued dominance of a totalitarian mentality.

The main theses of my paper are as follows:

1. In the first stage of Polish transformation from Communism to capitalism (market economy) an elitist type of democracy has emerged and the new political power elites have alienated themselves from society at all social levels.

2. This has caused a decline of confidence in the new post-Solidarity elites and the main political institutions.

3. A majority of the Polish society is willing to participate actively in the ongoing economic and social changes but such aspirations are being disregarded by the new political elites.

4. Due to "incapacitation" in past times, a majority of society is socially disintegrated and searching for good leaders (organizers of social life), i.e. people who could mobilize human resources to resolve local problems and keep citizens informed about local matters, since most citizens know nothing about budgets and means of reducing local fiscal budget strains.

5. Political preferences are widely dispersed among the population, ranging from leftist (although not extreme) to centrist to rightest. Rightist preferences are connected with a rejection of social equality and are held among the older as well as the younger generations. Social preferences for the majority of Poles are oriented toward the achievement of various freedoms, i.e. the emancipation from institutional limitations and the defence of individual rights, including the right to manage one's own private life, although the greater part of society is not oriented toward individualism.

6. In contrast to the American liberal and individualistic society, the majority of Poles are not involved in strong networks of voluntary associations. Thus, their expectations regarding democracy must aim at finding a compromise between the interests of different social groups (between interest groups as well as these groups and the various power elites) and an active role for the central and local governments in the resolution of social problems. This differs considerably, however, from

the current political practices of the new political elites, which do not appeal to the society for support.

7. Thus the main theoretical and practical issue of relevance for the next stage of transition is whether the new political elites will be able to find the appropriate means and methods to involve the various social groups in democratic decision-making and whether such authoritarian/totalitarian institutions as the Catholic Church and the bureaucratic state administration can give up their management of large sectors of social life. The implementation of ultra-liberalism in the economic sphere and the maintenance of social conservatism (totalitarian management of social life) leads to social schizophrenia and helps to sustain the deep division between those who rule ("them") and those who are the object of manipulation ("we"). It heightens the resistance of society to the capitalist means of reforming the Polish economy and engenders serious social conflicts and a growing apathy among many social groups. Thus, democracy might not be able to develop in an appropriate way in the near future. This dilemma shows also that the implementation of neoliberalism in Poland's economic and social life cannot proceed as it did in the United States or even in Latin American countries. Transformation from one economic and social system to a completely different one cannot be regarded as an easy "jump." It requires conscious efforts at involving the average citizenry in such a transformation. After all, the Polish society is not a society of illiterates and this is the end of the 20th century, not the end of the 19th century. Even if some apathy has emerged in widespread parts of society, new post-Solidarity political elites should take the responsibility for the future development of society, but not sidetable some matters or push society aside. This means developing a more participatory rather than elitist model of democracy. The question remains whether this implies populism or only responsibility to the future of Polish society.

Of course, these theses are to be taken as matters of discussion, not as authoritative claims. Although sociologists are not politicians and do not have sufficient clout to engage in political decision-making their discussions and "warning programs" may have an influence on the thoughts and actions of those in a position to make important decisions. Totalitarianism is an ever "attractive" alternative in such stormy, turning-point days as these.

These theses and their interpretations are based on the finds of sociological research I carried out recently (in March and April 1992) in five large Polish cities: Cracow, Poznan, Lodz, Katowice and Sosnowiec. This research was part of the international research program "Fiscal Austerity and Urban Innovation (FAUI) Project" coordinated by Prof. Dr. Terry Nichols Clark of the University of Chicago. The findings presented here are based on the second part of my research and deal with local self-governmental activity and the changing patterns of political culture in large Polish cities. Although the sample is not representative for the whole country (it is based on a quota-chance) sample which resulted in an over-representation of younger people--62% of my sample--and an over-representation of persons with a higher education--42.8% of the women, 53.9% of the men, or 46.1% of my sample), the findings can become a backdrop for a more general discussion of those passionate and dramatic problems of economic, political and social transformation.

Since young people will be the future "organizers" and "executors" involved in shaping social life, their convictions, opinions and preferences seem to me to be of great significance. As the findings of my research have shown, they can oppose the idea of a future Poland as a traditional and conservative society. Despite current conservative slogans and the practices of certain political and religious forces, these young people can really develop a new "open society" based on the standards of rational thinking and acting in the 21st century. Of course, this demands a conscious effort aimed at helping them to become more conscious rather than pushing them aside and making them helpless and subordinate to traditional, archaic institutions and ideas.

The methodological basis for my research was a questionnaire based partly on the FAUI questions, partly on questions and items used in various Polish sociological research in the past. The sample consisted of six social groups in each city--workers, representatives of the intelligentsia (physicians or teachers), students, secondary school pupils, businessmen and journalists--made up of 70-75 respondents in each city. The goal of such a selection was to choose those social groups which, on the one hand, are most representative of the current social structure in large cities and, on the other hand, can be seen as prospective "activists" in transforming society (especially youth, businessmen and journalists). The number of respondents--360 persons--is, in my opinion, sufficient to show general and more detailed aspects of the current transition period. Obviously, the findings and discussion presented here should be treated as preliminary. A more extensive discussion of these issues will be presented in a forthcoming monograph.

1. Confidence in political institutions and political leaders

Two years after the beginning of the Polish transformation toward a market economy and such significant political events as two free parliamentary elections, free autonomous local elections, and a presidential election--which were undeniable democratic practices--one may be surprised to find that the Polish society expresses a lack of confidence in the main political institutions and political leaders who are the most important symbols of the defeat of the Communist regime (see figure 1). Neither the new democratic parliament nor Solidarity and the new political parties, nor the President and his office enjoy the confidence of the greater part of society. The highest level of confidence, although low in percentage, is accorded to such long-existing institutions as the army, the press, the Catholic Church and the police. On the other hand, as a recent representative public opinion poll has shown (see figure 3), the general society holds the opinion that such institutions as the central government, parliament, labor unions and the President should have greater influence on the country's matters.

This inconsistency in the society's attitudes toward political and democratic institutions might be explained in terms of the past. As sociological research carried out in the past decades has shown, the Polish society expresses its lack of confidence in political institutions which are impersonal and perceived as bureaucratic; to the contrary, the majority of society expresses somewhat greater confidence in particular political leaders (although not in all, not even in those who became symbols of the overthrow of the Communist regime) in the past as in the present. As one of the well-known Polish sociologists, S. Nowak, put it, this is the opposition between the "world of institutions" and the "world of people." This personalization of political institutions, which are perceived through their leaders, is not a specific feature of Poland alone. However, in Poland the reception of political leaders in public consciousness is much more significant than in other countries. Having confidence and trust in people was always one of the important causes of support for public actions--social protest as well as general social activity. And if more than two-thirds of the society expresses its lack of confidence in people during this period of systemic transformation, the result is social conflict and the rejection of this method of economic transformation.

What has happened, then, to make the Polish society lose its confidence not only in political institutions, but also in its political leaders? According to opinion polls, the greatest level of confidence was placed in individuals not so closely associated with Solidarity, and much less confidence in the old Solidarity activists. This can be considered a "betrayal" of society by the Solidarity intellectuals.

Polish society has become disappointed and feels deceived by its former fighters for freedom from the Communist regime. These people are now perceived as fighting only for their own profits, and their efforts to make changes in the economy are perceived as contradictory to society's preferences and aspirations. It is certainly significant that more than 60% of the respondents state that a post-Solidarity

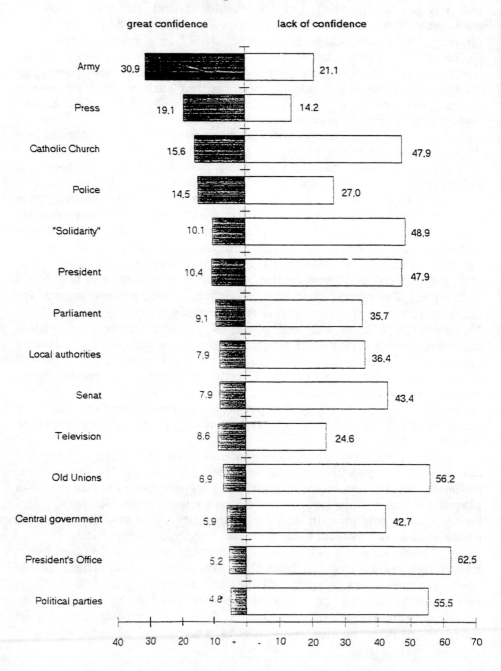

Figure 1: CITIZEN'S CONFIDENCE IN POLITICAL INSTITUTIONS
(total sample N=363, in %)

Figure 2: CITIZEN'S INTEREST IN POLITICS AND CONFIDENCE IN PEOPLE
(total sample. in %)

a. Interest in politics   b. Confidence in people

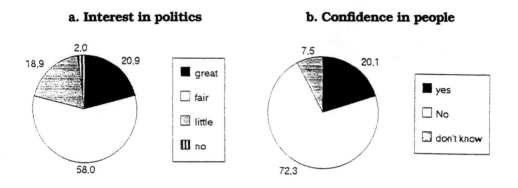

c. Which of the following institutions and organizations defends the average citizen's concerns the best?

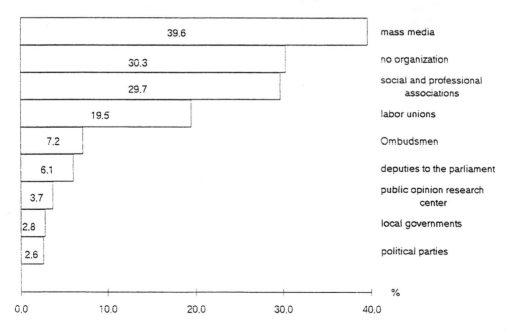

Figure 3: CITIZEN'S OPINIONS ABOUT DEMOCRACY (in %)

a. What is occuring in Poland now?

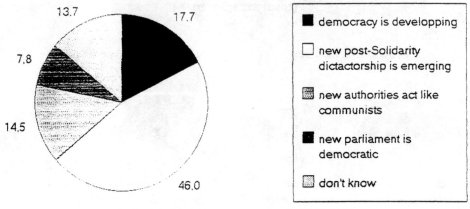

b. Is democracy necessary in Poland?

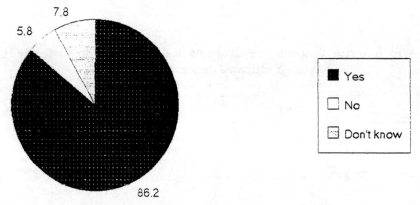

c. What democracy is

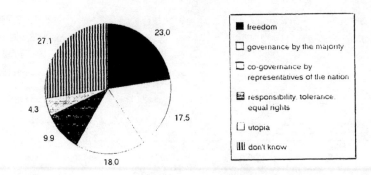

dictatorship is emerging in Poland and the new post-Solidarity elites act just like the Communists (see figure 3). This reply takes into account the political leaders as well as the parliamentary deputies. Significantly, many people expressed the opinion that the most important institutions trying to defend their interests are the press, the ombudsman and professional associations, but not the deputies in the democratically elected parliament (see figure 2).

This does not mean that the Polish society does not want a market economy; it wants it, but in a modern form and not with the conditions predominant in the 19th century such as high unemployment and a low standard of living (see table 1). Similarly, the Polish society rejects a subordination to the Catholic Church and wants democracy, not an elitist or closed form, but in a form based on joint problem solving. This involves cooperation between the new power elites and the various social groups. The currently perceived withdrawal of the post-Solidarity elite within their own circle is taken to be a "betrayal" of the society's interest in transforming the system on behalf of the entire society. Of course, one can claim that capitalism never develops on behalf of the entire society, but if it is coupled with democracy, then there should not be such an opposition between the preferences and aspirtations of the elite and those of the majority of society.

The findings of my research and public opinion polls show that Polish society opts strongly for developing democratic practices (over 80% positive response), even in view of the vicissitudes which are involved in the first stages. This may also been taken to be a desire for responsiveness and responsibility of the elite.

Thus political institutions and post-Solidarity leaders are perceived as acting against the interests of a majority of the society. This is the opinion not only of one but the majority of the social groups. Of course, there are some differences to be found between various communities (cities) with their varying socio-economic conditions. In cities with the greatest disturbances from the economic transformation and its drastic social consequences, social confidence in post-Solidarity elites and political institutions is much lower (for example, L<dŒ, Katowice and Sosniwiec) than in other cities which did not suffer such drastic disturbances (for example, Poznan and Cracow). However, even in these cities a certain amount of anxiety is evident, showing that the economic transformation has an effect on everyone.

The latest events in 1992 (beginning with the strikes in January through to the political quarrels between the post-Solidarity parties during the creation of the new "wider parliamentary coalition" and the attempted negotiations between the labor union Solidarity and the government) have shown that it was not wise to neglect certain matters

Table 1: SELF-EVALUATION OF THE FAMILY BUDGETS IN 1991
(representative panel sample, in %)

	Households					
	Total 1991		February 1991		November 1991	
			place of residence		place of residence	
	Febr.	Nov.	town	village	town	village
We do not have enough money even for elementary everyday needs	7.5	10.8	7.0	8.5	9.7	13.4
We have money only for the cheapest food and basic expenses	26.9	28.8	26.4	28.1	28.8	30.4
We live very economically to fulfil basic needs	37.3	42.7	35.3	41.9	43.0	41.9
We live economically and have enough money	22.8	14.2	24.9	18.1	16.0	10.1
We have enough money to live without making economies	4.2	2.0	4.8	3.0	2.1	1.8
We live another way	1.3	1.5	1.6	0.4	1.2	2.4

Source: K. Karcz, Z. Kedzior: An accumulation of the Threats. "Economic life"
("Zycie Gospodarcze"). 9. February 1992. p. 19
Note: Average salary reached 170 dollars per month at the end of 1991

at the beginning of the transformation, but had negative effects. The lack of a well-developed system of information dissemination, irresponsible promises and the claim of a "decommunisation" of society have produced disorientation for many in the society. The result was a rejection of political participation of the majority in the parliamentary election in October 1991 (60% abstinence). Nevertheless, the majority of my respondents expressed a great interest in politics (80% in figure 2) and demanded more cooperation among the elites, but also the opportunity for more active participation in the ongoing transformation. The Polish society has strongly expressed its desire to be taken seriously. Will the post-Solidarity elites be able to turn to society and offer it's citizens great involvement? Elitist democracy cannot mean pushing society aside without becoming an oligarchy rather than a democracy. Even if a great part of the Polish society expresses its demand for a strong leader (nearly 59% of my respondents), this does mean that a dictatorship is desired. There is rather a desire for a good "householder", a good organizer of social life, and an orientation toward more cooperation than competition. How then can capitalism (market economy) be developed in such a society? In any case, each society possesses its own special features and the methods of its transformation must be adapted to it, not implemented "blindly."

These are not academic questions, since models of great participation and democratic practices have been developed in other countries with good results and could been taken into account. Decentralization of power, regionalization and more autonomy for local community's economic and social decision-making could be a more efficient way to reach market economy and democracy. This might result, too, in more confidence in local political institutions and elites, if the local authorities were more responsible for the actual transformation in their local communities. The present "incapacitation" of local governments (as the first stage of my research has shown) resulted through the internal fighting of elites over their own profits, rather than from problem solving. If there is little room left to local leaders, citizens may also feel "incapacitated" or tend to act only on their own selfish and particular interests (which also leads to pathological individual and group behavior).

Finally, it is worth stressing that the majority of my respondents (69%) demand an active role for central and local governments in the search for new possibilities and methods for transforming the economy. Although there were more supporters of a continuity of the current neoliberal strategy (51%), supporters of a new method for economic transformation were also considerable (38%). This reflects a considerable polarization of opinion about the future transformation of economy and society, and one can assume, will bring strong social conflicts and protests in the next stages of transition. Thus, so much depends on the actions to be taken by the new power elites in terms of seeking involvement by society. Finally it should be mentioned that there is a long Polish tradition of assuming responsibility for the whole nation and state. The individualistic, ultra-liberal style of capitalism (more American than European) may bring more negative than positive results in the case of Poland.

2. Citizen's opinions about democracy, civil rights and freedom

Although democracy is perceived as a desirable goal for Poland, about one-third of the respondents in my research do not know exactly what democracy means and involves (see figure 3). One of the respondents replied, for instance, "Walesa still speaks about democracy and democracy, but what is it?". It is not the fault of the people that they do not know. It is rather a great error of the new political elites that they do not help society to learn the meaning of democracy. Of course, since the Polish society is not a society of illiterates and modern mass media are widely available (television, press, radio), a majority of the society does understand what is involved in a democracy.

As I have shown in previous writings, three meanings of democracy are currently circulating in Poland, which are also found in countries with long-standing democracies. 1. Democracy is held to be a form of ruling the country, where decisions are made by the majority while taking into account the rights of minorities (17% of the respondents); 2. democracy considered a method of cooperation between elites and citizens (not the masses), meditated via freely elected representatives (18%); 3. democracy is associated with the idea of freedom (23%). For nearly 10% of the respondents, democracy also means taking responsibility for the vicissitudes of society, showing tolerance in human relations, granting equal rights and social justice to all. (see figure 3). The first meaning mentioned above reflects a more elitist way of thinking; the second a more participatory model of democracy (albeit there are no "clear" models of democracy in social reality); the third stresses the rights of individuals to create their own life paths as opposed to submitting to hierarchical and authoritarian social institutions. The individualistic meaning of democracy is not the same as in the American society, but it shows that Polish society strongly opts for the protection of individual civil rights as a basis for a democratic political and social system (a somewhat similar type of democracy was proposed by S. Ossowski, one of the well-known Polish sociologists in the 1960s). Although only 4% of the respondents did not believe that democracy can be achieved, nobody defined democracy as a kind of elitist game among a few people who claim to rule over others. The process of learning what an elitist type democracy is will be very painful and disappointing for many Poles. This can already be observed now during and after the collapse of the idea of a "great post-Solidarity coalition.

Nevertheless, the most significant factors today in Poland's period of transition from totalitarianism to democracy is the mounting aspiration toward personal freedom (nearly 40% of the respondents) and the near rejection of social equality as a basic social principle (only 5.5% of the respondents supported social equality as the main social principle, although 52% was of the opinion that personal freedom and social equality are important to the same degree. This is especially evident among the young and representatives of the intelligentsia. It can be understood as acceptance of the modern form of democracy, i.e. the welfare state. The orientation towards personal freedom is especially evident in the preferences for different types of freedoms (figure 4). The most desired freedom is the choice of where to live and travel (for nearly 60%); secondly, the freedom of information (for 49%); and thirdly, the freedom of religion (45%), which indicates a great anxiety present in the society today about pressure from the Catholic Church and efforts to subordinate society to dogmatic religious doctrines). It is also significant in this first stage of Polish transformation that only for 9% of my respondents freedom involved the opportunity to join labor unions and voluntary associations or help to create a political party (7.2%). This reveals that the Polish society is still "not organized," it means that there still exists a "social void" between the state organs and the society. However, for 17%, freedom to vote is appreciated as an important matter. Similarly, the freedom found one's own business was important for 24% of the respondents. Since the "freedom to..." is becoming an important matter in shaping one's own life conditions, this means that a democratic mentality is emerging dynamically in Polish society.

Nevertheless, since more than 60% of the respondents stated that the most important aspect of the current transformation is "freedom from..." and not so much "freedom to...", it is clear that the transition is just beginning and it will take a long time to begin organizing and managing different social and individual possibilities for "taking one's fate in one's own hands." This is particularly so in face of the current state of growing unemployment and declining social status. Moreover, more than 50% of the respondents is of the opinion that the division between rich and poor will continue to exist. This may in turn help to sustain apathetic and resigned attitudes toward shaping one's own personal and social life, thus making it difficult to develop democratic

Figure 4: CITIZEN'S OPINIONS ABOUT FREEDOMS (in %)

a. What is the most important kind of freedom?

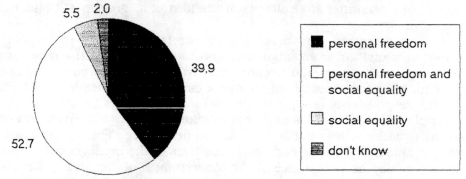

b. Which of the following convictions do you hold?

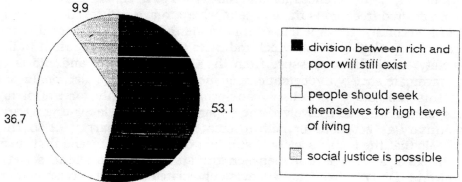

c. A choice of particular civil liberties

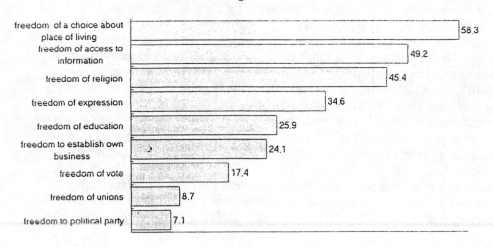

patterns at the local level. It may also lead individuals to concentrate on their own particularistic, selfish matters (separable goods) and shy away from seeking a common basis for the resolution of local problems.

Table 2: CITIZEN'S OPINIONS ABOUT THEIR OWN POLITICAL IMPACT

Question: "If local government intended to implement a project you think is wrong, what could you do in this matter?"

NEGATIVE RESPONSES	Number	%
1. Local government does not need citizens' opinions	82	22,5
2. It is not the custom consult citizens	115	31,6
3. The voice of an individual is meaningless	149	41,0
4. I am too insignificant a person to be taken into account	59	16,2
5. Citizens are afraid of speaking in public about local matters	37	10,1
TOTAL NEGATIVE RESPONSES (of all the responses)	442	51,2
POSITIVE RESPONSES	Number	%
6. If citizens would create protest groups, they could influence local government decision making	118	32,5
7. If individual citizens or their groups are active, they can influence local government	42	11,5
8. Citizens may appeal to the intervention of elected deputies in this city	35	9,6
9. Citizens may address regional or national authorities	13	3,5
10. Citizens should turn to local mass-media to press local government to change wrong decision	94	25,9
11. Citizens may influence local government through political parties or other pressure groups	41	11,2
12. Citizens may petition local government to change wrong decision	61	16,8
13. Citizens may influence local government through informal contacts with councilpersons or board	16	4,4
TOTAL POSITIVE RESPONSES (of all the responses)	420	48,7

        More than one-third is of the opinion that people should strive
for a high standard of living by themselves (figure 4). This is especially
true among the young and businessmen. Entrepreneurial attitudes are
quite widespread in Polish society, although mostly in terms of
personal, selfish desires in this first stage of "building" capitalism.
Nevertheless, as my research has shown, a desire to participate in
common community life and resolve local problems is indeed
appreciated by a great part of the average citizenry (see table 2). They are
looking for and expecting new dynamic leaders at the local level who
could mobilize them to take part in common actions. And they are very
disappointed that "Solidarity" activists did not become such local
leaders or organizers, but fought instead for their own profits alone.

        Another dramatic change in social consciousness and the system
of values can be witnessed in the opinion that social justice is nearly
impossible to reach (only 9% is of the opinion that it is possible).

        Thus in this first period of transition from Communism to
capitalism and democracy, the main and most dramatic changes can be
found in the social mentality: in the rejection of the basic principles of
Communism (especially the basic principle of social equality) and an
orientation towards freedom. But, to be less optimistic, this freedom-
oriented people is on the one hand highly disoriented and on the other
hand requests submission to institutional order. This can be seen not
only in the rejection of submission to the Catholic Church's hierarchical
aspirations, but also to the state law. Significantly, nearly 40% of the
respondents, regardless of the city, gave its consent to the idea that
politicians may break laws in some circumstances. In other words,
many Poles stand on the verge of anarchy (see figure 5).

        In viewing the issues of social liberalism vs. conservatism, the
opinions of my respondents show that a great part of Polish society
strongly oppose current conservative actions of the new political elites
and the Catholic Church. It is especially surprising that in such a
predominantly Catholic country, more than 80% of the people living in
big cities (although less of those living in small towns and villages) is
against the domination of the Catholic Church in social life; more than
90% (of my sample, albeit only 55% of the country) support the
legalization of abortion. It is quite evident that submission to such an
authoritarian/totalitarian institution as the Catholic Church is much
stronger in small communities than in larger cities. In the latter, more
heterogeneity generates more tolerant and liberal orientations towards
moral issues. Similarly, more social liberalism can be found in cities in
terms of such issues as equal opportunity for working women (90% in
the cities included in my investigation, but only 33% in a nationwide
poll--a liberal- conservative gap which may be one of the most

significant barriers to developing modern, open and democratic minded society. Similar results were found in the question of sex education in school and participation in public affairs.

Continuity of some aspects of social mentality can also be seen in regard to the relation between State responsibility for meeting social needs and the individual's own responsibilities. 70% of the respondents in my sample and 66% in a representative nation-wide sample were against drastic cuts in the central budget on social needs, such as education, health protection and prisioners' funds. This indicates that the current level of social security is so long that citizen's strongly oppose any further lowering. Privatization of public health and education will lead to a deeper division between those who have the opportunities to fulfill their own needs and those who cannot maintain their current level of individual and family security. This deep division may be seen as a throwback to the earliest stages of capitalism, similar to conditions in the 19th century.

Changes in social mentality and a system of values can also be found in terms of citizen's electoral behavior and political preferences, although continuity is to be observed regarding basic individual life values.

3. Citizens' electoral behaviors, political preferences and individual life values

Transformation from Communism to capitalism and democracy is also a matter of people's practical behavior, not only their convictions, opinions and statements.

As the analyses of the electoral behavior of Poles done in the past three years have shown, the greatest turnout can be found among the intelligentsia and peasants, much lower (after the first free parliamentary election in 1989) among workers and youth. My findings confirm this, with 70% of the intelligentsia report having votes, but only 45% of the workers. The intelligentsia voted mainly for the Democratic Union and the Liberal-Democratic Congress, while the workers voted for "Solidarity" and the Confederation of Independent Poland.

This is not a surprising division. Firstly because the intelligentsia is much more interested in politics and particular parties and leaders. Secondly because Solidarity was a manifestation of workers' political aspirations and it was believed that Solidarity activists would act for the workers' interests. When workers reported that Solidarity activists betrayed them, then they voted for the Confederation of Independent Poland, in spite of its demagogic, irresponsible promises.

Figure 5: a. Attitudes to rules being broken by politicians

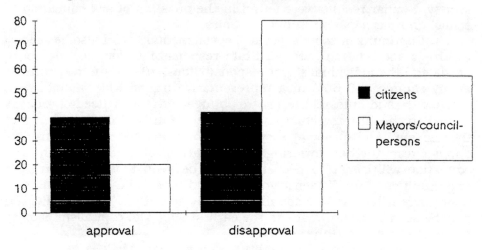

b. Attitude towards legalization of abortion

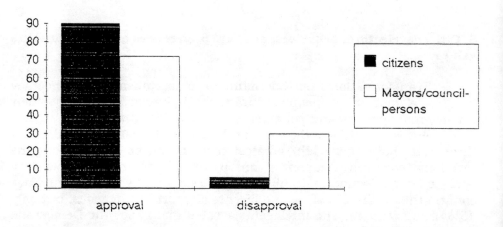

The disappointment of workers in Solidarity as an organization and in its activists resulted, paradoxically, in impetuous attempts of the top echelons of Solidarity to mobilize support from workers and other employees. This could be seen in the January 1992 strikes, in the continuous pressure of Solidarity on the government and in attempts to mobilize mass protests. Nonetheless a large part of the workers lost their confidence in Solidarity, although the actual numbers vary considerable between communities.

The present great turmoil in the economy and society is causing great polarization of political preferences and orientations among many Poles. Although leftist and centrist preferences and orientations are still visible (52% of my sample), nearly 40% expressed a rightest orientation, especially young people and women. The middle-aged, especially those who lost the most through the present transformation, expressed leftist and centrist orientations. It is not surprising, obviously, that in the cities with the greatest economic disturbances, more leftist orientation appeared, but also more rightest (especially Cracow and Lodz). These cities have at present the worst economic and social situations, causing, as in many other countries, a polarization of citizens.

However, the rise of a rightest orientation, surprisingly, does not mean a traditional rightist, conservative value orientation in the case of the majority of Poles. As I showed above, a majority of Poles (at least those in the cities surveyed) express social liberalism regarding main social issues and demands the active role of central and local governments in resolving social problems. Their rightist orientation, in my opinion, demonstrates itself in a rejection of social equality as a basic social life principle and favoring of different types of individual freedoms. Thus these people oppose the Catholic Church's aspirations to rule society on the one hand, and support a deep division between the material and financial situation of individuals and families on the other hand. They still believe that their own efforts to shape their own life conditions can be sufficient and the help and support of others unnecessary. On the one hand, this can lead to dynamizing social changes toward market economy, but on the other it leads, as the everyday examples show, to pathological, aggressive and unscrupulous actions against other people, individuals and social groups. It causes insecurity in social life to develop and prevents progress beyond the early stage of capitalism formation, thus bringing more negative than positive results (more indifference and aggression) for social development.

Nevertheless, Polish society continues to grant great significance to family and social groups of reference (figure 6). And since a great part of my sample consisted of younger people, the values of professional skills and education were much appreciated. It may a good prognosis of the orientation of the new generation toward building more modern capitalism and not submitting to traditional, archaic ways of thinking and acting. Since this new generation also seeks more information about politics, economic issues and claims to finding ways to shape its own life, one can expect that in spite of the totalitarian aspirations of the Catholic hierarchy and Catholic politicians, these young people will be able to create a modern, open and democratic society.

Figure 6: CITIZEN'S VALUE-ORIENTATIONS, REFERENCE GROUPS AND RELIGIOUS ACTIVITIES (in%)

a. Value-orientations

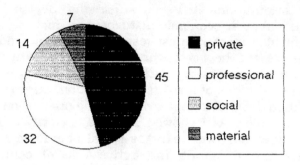

b. Means to achieve individual life goals

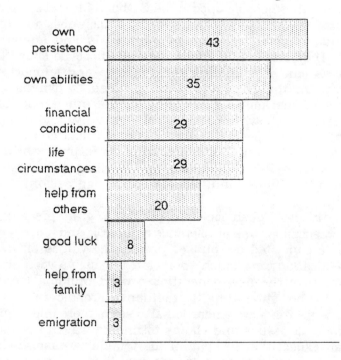

c. Citizen's reference groups

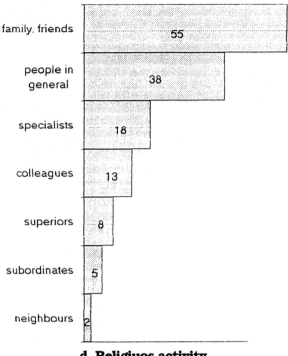

d. Religiuos activity

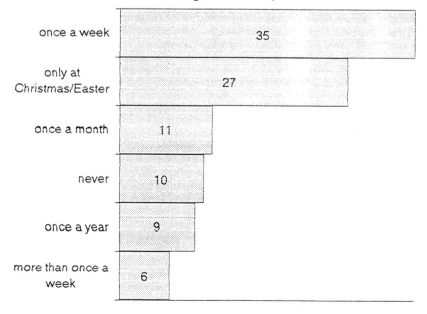

Of course, great efforts are needed to take advantage of the high professional skills, rather than pushing them into unemployment (at present 63% of the unemployed are under 35 years of age). This difficult situation for young people has an influence on its turn toward materialistic values.

4.The materialist-postmaterialist dimension and values

In general, both the mayors or councilpersons and the citizens of the five large cities surveyed in my research expressed a strongly materialistic orientation (see figure 7). This is understandable in view of the deep economic recession, rising unemployment, the indefinite future and the sinking standard of living.

However, even in this situation 20% of those surveyed expressed a post-materialist orientation, i.e. toward issues involving active participation at the local community level, such as having more say at work or in political matters. This shows that a portion of the Poles has not given up hope of shaping a new way of life and better social conditions. If the new political elite does not become a closed circle, the citizens could become involved in attempts to achieve the Polish aspiration of becoming part of modern Europe.

Since the transformation of the economy depends more on governmental and managerial efforts, citizens expect a more active governmental role in preventing the economic decline. Thus economic issues are given top priority, followed by such issues as crime prevention and maintenance of social order. The present lack of precisely defined legal basis for the new social situation is seen as a threat to basic life conditions by a great part of society. Of course, one can claim that is the necessary price for a fundamental transformation of society, but it also results in serious destruction of the psychological powers of endurance in many people. The clear resistance of the Polish society to the Latin American model of economic transformation with its destruction of social fabric and ties, should be taken into account not only by politicians and economists, but also be their foreign advisors.

Figure 7: MATERIALIST-POST-MATERIALIST DIMENSION

a. In general

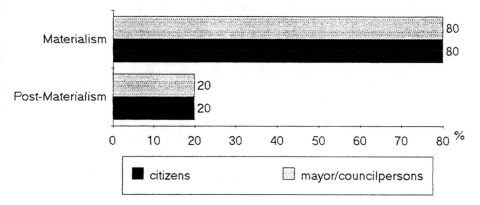

b. Particular concerns in materialist-post-materialist dimension

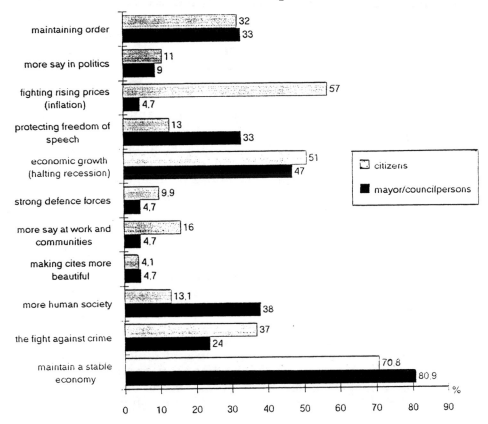

Thus, there should be great efforts undertaken to teach people a new outlook based not on Christianity but on a universal ethic which emphasizes the responsibility of all individuals, all social groups, political parties and their leaders for these basic conditions of life. If thePolish society is to become modern, not neocolonial, not half slavish, changes in the mentality of individuals and groups must appear quickly. But who is to ensure that it does?

Democracy means not only taking responsibility for one's own life, but also for the future of society as a whole. Thus the American, individualistic way of capitalistic development which is being imposed now on post-communist countries (and so clearly accepted in Poland) may bring more negative effects for Polish society in the future.

And indeed, many Poles are of the opinion that joint attempts by local authorities to mobilize human resources may bring more effective and favorable results than the decisions being made centrally by the political elite.

5. Dilemmas of the present and future systemic transformation

As recent political and social events have shown (strikes, collapse of formatting wide parliamentary coalition, mass protests), the lack of a clear vision of the future for Poland's economy and society is a real threat to the chances of democracy developing in Poland. Even the creation of a pluralistic system of political parties, which is perceived as the basis for a democratic political system, cannot be considered progress toward democracy if the political leaders fight only for their own profit, i.e. for their share of power. The splitting of the Solidarity movement into distinct "political families" led to similar divisions in society, as seen in the appearance of various political orientations, but it did not lead to a crystalization of clear political programs for the coming social transition. On the contrary, it led to personal quarrels and fights over materials goods and higher political positions.

This has led to an alienation of post-Solidarity elite at all levels of society and a disappointment in democratic institutions and leaders. Similarly, strong opposition between the elites and a majority of society has surfaced on the issue of the future steps toward economic transformation and the issue of popular participation in the implementing social and economic changes.

All of the problems outlined in the previous sections of this paper show not only the enormous complication and difficulties involved in transforming the economy and society, but that the implementation of the American model of an ultra-liberal economic sphere and a conservative social sphere does not work in the Polish context.

In my opinion, the conscious action and thinking of various social groups (not only workers, intelligentsia but also the peasants) developed over the past decade is a factor in the present rejection of certain stages of capital formation which were typical of the 19th century.

This brings new dilemmas and contradictions to bear on the coming period of transition toward market economy and democracy. First, it is to be questioned whether economic transformation must be implemented by destroying the existing economic fabric of society. Second, it is to be questioned whether the elitist type of democratic practice and decision-making is the best path for Poland in view of the Latin American experience of economic transformation with the support of the International Monetary Fund and the World Bank in the late 1970s and 1980s.

Another issue is the role of education in the transformation of society. In which direction? Should it support the submission of society to Catholicism and to the idea of a deep division between the rich and the poor? Or toward modern education based on rational thinking and the development of highly skilled specialists who can develop the Polish economic and social life.

One of the most thorny issues at the present stage of transformation is the privatization of health protection services. Because of the low income level of a majority of families, this can have severely negative consequences for a great part of society. Can health protection be left to market forces at this time? Is this a responsible way of general social security at the end of the 20th century?

The same type of questions can be raised in regard to the protection of the natural environment. In spite of a great awareness among part of the population, the ultra-liberalism implemented nearly three years ago has already had negative consequences. And, significantly, the economic recession has forced ecological problems out of the current public opinion. Average citizens are so much engaged in defending their material and financial living conditions that they do not concern themselves with improving the natural environment.

Finally, I would like to stress the great importance of more participation in local problem solving. Recent events of hatred and intolerance in some communities show how important it is that responsible groups and individual join forces. If aggression continues to mount, democracy will not develop as a real practice but will be only a mask covering up social synicism, hypocrisy and hatred. Political democracy based on a pluralism of political parties is not sufficient grounds to say that real democracy is developing. It may help instead to generate a pseudo-democracy or a kind of political hypocrisy.

Thus the dilemmas and contradictions which have emerged in the wake of the first transitional period in Poland are connected not only with a problem of a method of economic transformation and its social consequences, but also with problems of transforming society-- social consciousness, mentality, everyday behavior and responsibility for not individual living conditions but also those in the local community and the society as a whole.

The theoretical lesson to be learned from this first period of the "Great Transformation" involves the question whether Poland will have to repeat the early stage of capitalism formation with all its negative social consequences or whether there will be a "Polish way to capitalism" based not on destruction, even "creative destruction", but on "creative adaptation. This requires, of course, more conscious thinking about the future and more responsibility being borne for the fate of the entire society (although not in the Communist manner) and fighting over power and privileges for the sake of personal ambition. Will this be possible in Poland?

6

CULTURAL MINORITIES AND MAJORITY RULE[1]

Janusz Mucha
Department of Sociology, University of Gdańsk

The aim of this paper is to present some ramifications of the recent democratization process in Poland. The paper will concentrate on the relations between the new politically and culturally dominant group and various cultural minorities. It is to show similarities and differences between the three levels of these relations: institutional, semi-institutional and the level of collective behavior.

Democracy, in its simple and textbook sense, is a form of government in which it is recognized that the ultimate authority belongs to the people, and the people have the right to participate in the decision-making process and to appoint and dismiss those who rule. For Robert A. Dahl, one of the leading scholars dealing with the theory of democracy, the "key characteristic of democracy is the continuing responsiveness of

---

[1] The problems presented in this text are discussed in a much more elaborate and documented way in my paper "Democratization and Cultural Minorities. Polish Case of the 1980/90s", to be published in *East European Quarterly* in 1992.

the government to the preferences of its citizens, considered as political equals."[2]

Democratization is a process of transition from an undemocratic (authoritarian, totalitarian) to a more democratic system. This process may be controlled but may also be uncontrolled by the ruling group of the outgoing regime. The recent example of the uncontrolled process is the situation in Poland.

Both democracy and democratization have not only political, but also economic, social and cultural meanings. Cultural democracy is, for the purpose of this paper, a social situation in which cultural values and norms of the majority of the population are being publicly accepted and expressed. Cultural democratization would thus be a process of transition in which these values are becoming more public and overtly appreciated. People who believe in these values and norms are being allowed to organize themselves freely and to participate in public life as their "bearers." Religious and ideological values and norms are obviously a legitimate element of culture and will be discussed in this paper.

If one agrees that the right of public contention is a crucial aspect of political democracy, one should apply a similar rule to cultural democracy. In the full sense of the word, it would mean the right of cultural minorities to express freely and publicly their own beliefs and value systems.

In this paper, I will analyze the recent situation of cultural minorities in Poland. What is "minority group?" Louis Wirth's classic definition refers to it as "a group of people who, because of their physical or cultural characteristics, are singled out from the others in the society in which they live for differential and unequal treatment, and who therefore regard themselves as objects of collective discrimination." [3]The existence of minority groups implies the existence of a "majority group." In this paper, the term "majority" will be used only in the numerical sense, otherwise the term "dominant group" will be used. By minorities, the suppressed groups as defined above is to be understood.

Unlike the Polish society between the two world wars, i.e. a religiously and politically pluralistic society, post-war Poland was, during the decades of the Communist system, highly "homogeneous" at least on the surface of public life. During the interwar period, ethnic minorities constituted about one-third of the population; after the war, they constituted only about 5% of the total. Similar numbers are found

---

[2]See Robert A. Dahl, PolYarchy. Participation and Opposition. New Haven and London: Yale University Press 1971, p. 1. See also, among his other books, Democracy and Its Critics. New Haven and London, : Yale University Press 1989.

[3]Louis Wirth, "The Problem of Minority Groups'" in The Science of Man in the World Crisis, edited by Ralph Linton, New York: Columbia University Press 1945, p. 347.

for religion. Before World War II, nearly one-third of the population had a non-Roman Catholic background, while today this proportion does not exceed five percent. Before the war many parties operated in Poland. During the Communist regime, there were officially three political parties, but the leading role of the Communist Party was a fundamental political principle. The government did not tolerate opposition. Political homogeneity was based on oppression.

The Roman Catholic Church has been considered by the majority of the Poles to be the guardian of the national heritage and the continuation of national tradition. This tradition has been valued very highly by Poles. According to the beliefs of this majority group, to be a good Pole means to be a member of the Roman Catholic Church or, at least, to believe in God. The official Communist ideology, based on Marxism-Leninism, was of an anti-religious character. The political authorities strongly criticized the Catholic values and norms.

After decades of socialist socialization, more Poles came to believe in some socialist values (justice, equality, welfare state), but they never accepted Communism as a supreme value.

The normative system, have been propaged in Poland during the Communist period, did not reflect the beliefs of the majority of Poles. Therefore, we can say that not only a political but also a cultural democracy was missing in Poland.

The Poles attempted several times to change the over all (both political and cultural) system and to democratize it. These attempts on the part of the majority of society became successful at the end of the 1980s. It would be difficult to question the democratic character of the current political system.

How has the situation of cultural minorities changed? During the interwar period, about 15% of the population in Poland were Ukrainians. They had full citizens' rights and were represented in Parliament by various political parties. However, the Ukrainians were under very strong pressure to assimilate into the Polish majority. They demanded cultural autonomy, but were never granted it. Jews constituted another large minority. Nearly 10% of the population of Poland was Yiddish-speaking Jews. There were no efforts to assimilate them, but rather to isolate them. Relations between these minorities and the dominant society were never good. There were also religious tensions in Poland, particularly between the members of the two branches of the Catholic Church--the dominant Latin (Roman) and the Greek (Uniate or Ukrainian) Church.

During World War II, the German occupation and the Holocaust, nearly the total Jewish population of Poland was exterminated. However, among the Communists who were sent by the Soviet Union to

Poland at the end of the war in order to establish a new political system, the percentage of Jews was very high. Extermination of the Jews would probably have made the attitude of the Poles toward the remnants of the Jewish population much more sympathetic than before the war, but their link with the new regime prevented this change. The Jews were not labeled victims who needed help but were instead Communists, i.e. aliens who used to live on the peripheries of Polish society and now suddenly had become a part of the politically dominant and socially unaccepted group. Much later, the anti-Jewish sentiments were supported very strongly by the Communist authorities.

The hatred between the Poles and the Ukrainians resulted from the latter's collaboration with the German occupants during the war. After the war, when the Polish military administration displaced about 200,000 "Polish" Ukrainians from their own territories in the eastern part of Poland to the northern and western part of the country, the Polish population did not protest. The situation of the Uniate Church in post-war Poland was in a practical sense very difficult. Political authorities transferred many church buildings either to the Russian Orthodox or to the Roman Catholic Church. The Uniate Church became practically an underground religious movement for nearly forty years.

Soon after the war, the territory of Poland was shifted about 150 miles westward. Poland gained regions in which millions of Germans had lived earlier. Most of them fled westward during the war, but the rest was, according to international agreements, but forcefully, displaced to Germany after the war. According to the Polish state authorities, no Germans stayed in Poland. This is not true. In 1956, in the 1970s and in the 1980s, many people were allowed to leave Poland for Germany if they claimed German nationality. However, German Poles were denied the right to establish their own cultural associations and to use the German language in schools. On the other hand, an atmosphere of "German peril", jeopardizing the post-war international arrangements (particularly borders) was created by Polish authorities.

Besides national groups, like Ukrainians, Jews and Germans, one can also mention another cultural minority: the unbelievers. They will NOT be defined here as people who are only superficially religious under the influence of anti-clerical ideology, and have a pro-choice as opposed to pro-life attitude, if they declare that they believe in God. Unbelievers will be understood here as those people who declare that they do not believe in God. The definition will have a philosophical rather than a sociological character. Therefore, unbelievers constitute a social aggregate and not a social group in strong, sociological sense.

There are some social problems that most of the non-believers face in a predominantly Catholic environment, problems that could have united them. They prefer, however, to remain invisible rather than to organize themselves. It is interesting that the political authorities, so deeply involved in the atheistic campaign, also wanted the "independent" unbelievers to be invisible.

Non-believers in Poland operate within the context of the Catholic "majority society." Everybody who is not Catholic, and particularly who does not believe in God, is an alien, an alien who cannot be eliminated but potentially can and should be transformed into a member of the dominant group. In this situation, unbelievers who manifest their attitudes find themselves subjected to a strong social control. Actually, they must give up most of the ways of behavior they would otherwise prefer.

The political context is very important here. Not all unbelievers, probably only a slight minority of them, were supporters of Communism. The Communist Party claimed, however, the monopoly of representation of their interests. Unbelievers who did not consider themselves Communists, were manipulated by the ruling group, and, moreover, treated as Communists by the religious majority.

Throughout the whole Communist period of Polish history, non-believers constituted an aggregate that was, paradoxically, in cultural terms discriminated against. However, in a certain political sense, some of them belonged to a dominant collectivity.

To sum up this part of the paper, the Communist political system did not guarantee the majority a chance to express itself on many matters without fear of reprisal. At the same time, the system monopolized the representation of some minorities and prevented them from taking care of their own interests and did not guarantee other minorities a chance to express themselves. We could even say that the long-lasting and relatively strong tensions and conflicts were supported by the Communist authorities.

The late 1980s, and particularly the turn of the decade, brought cultural and political democratization. How did the situation of the Polish cultural minorities change? Obviously, it has many aspects. Let us take a look at some of them. The first will be called institutional. We will be interested here in the political decision-making process.

As a consequence of the political attitudes of new political leadership, a representative of the Ukrainian group was elected a member of Parliament. Some ethnic minorities elected their representatives to the local councils in regions where they dominated numerically. The Jewish contribution to the Polish culture became officially recognized; after 30 years, the first rabbi was appointed; festivals of Jewish culture were being sponsored and organized. Official diplomatic relationships with the state of Israel were resumed after more than 20 years of suspension. The authorities allowed the registration of cultural associations of German Poles in various western regions of the country. The Parliament appointed the Ethnic Minorities Committees in both of its chambers.

The hierarchy of the Roman Catholic Church decided to return at least some of the church buildings which legally belonged to the Uniate parishes, and had been transferred to it by the Communist authorities just after World War II.

On the institutional level, the situation of many minorities has improved. What has not improved is the situation of the minority of unbelievers. The new political system fully recognized the right of the overwhelming Roman Catholic cultural majority to express its preferences. The majority took complete advantage of this situation. Being responsive to the preferences of its citizenry, the new government decided to break with the old rule of separation of state and religion. Following the call of the bishops, a new regulation was issued by the Minister of National Education, effective 1 September 1990, that introduced religious education in all public schools at the primary and secondary level.

From the institutional point of view, relations between the cultural majority and the cultural minorities cannot be described as conflictual in the proper sense of the word. The ethnic and religious minorities which can be called "demanding minorities" here presented their needs and those needs were later fulfilled. No conflict occurred. Unbelievers, whom we can call a "retreatist minority," did not oppose decisions unfavorable to them, so a conflict did not emerge either.

The "demanding minorities" had access to at least some resources--material, organizational and symbolic. They could at least claim legitimacy of their demands. The "retreatist minority" had no or nearly no access to such resources, and its potential demands had no legitimacy in Polish society.

Institutional aspects overlap with societal aspects. The most important area where they meet is the Parliament. This is not only the supreme decision-making body but also a forum in which the opinions of various social groups are presented and discussed. Another area of this kind was the National Committee of the Solidarity Trade Union. Public statements of high-ranking government officials would also belong to this shadow category, as long as they are not being translated into political decisions. Let me give some examples.

In their capacities as members of Parliament, leaders of right-wing nationalistic parties had presented statements directed against some ethnic minorities and called for the strengthening of the public role of the Roman Catholic Church. Mr. Lech Walesa, in his capacity as presidential candidate and chairman of the Solidarity Trade Union, declared at the end of 1990 that it was not wrong to demand that Polish Jews publicly declare their ethnic background. He explained later that was against any kind of chauvinism and anti-semitism and that he had only meant that everybody should be proud of his or her ethnicity and that ethnic differences, since they existed, should not be hidden. The Polish Jews (probably only a few thousand now) recalled how they or their parents had been forced to wear the Star of David and were shot if caught without it during the Nazi regime.

The atheists became another target of the cultural majority. The abortion issue became highly publicized and politicized and the pro-choice attitude became identified by the pro-life activists with an atheist philosophy. At the beginning of 1991, the Deputy Prosecutor General issued a statement linking the economic, social and political troubles of Poland with the very presence of non-believers in the country.

Another example of an semi-institutional approach to a cultural (ideological) minority is the election program of some quite strong new political groups, demanding that the not-yet-existing Parliament pass a law forbidding the activists of the former Communist Party to hold any public offices during the next ten years. If the idea had been implemented (as it was late in Czechoslavakia), it would have meant that several hundred thousand people would be deprived of their citizens' rights because of their former political (and not criminal, at least from the formal point of view) activities. The semi-institutional and public approach to the members of the former Communist Party justifies, in my understanding, their analysis in terms of a political and ideological minority.

The non-institutional sphere of collective attitudes and actions is also extremely important for the democratization processes. They reflect the long-lasting cultural and political socialization of the Poles. They constitute also a background of many semi-institutional actions mentioned in the previous paragraphs.

Two examples will be discussed here. The first is the situation of the German ethnic minority. Until 1989, the Ministry of Interior, as well as the courts of justice, denied the existence of this group. Popular attitudes of Poles were also against any kind of legalization of German activities in Poland. The official situation changed after the 1989 parliamentary elections. Many German-Polish organizations have since been registered and the right of German Poles to develop their ethnic culture, to use the German language in many public places, was legally recognized. It did not change the popular mood. The ethnic tensions in Silesia that had been nearly completely hidden for 40 years, emerged with unprecedented strength. The Germans hoped to get the support from a Germany on the verge of unification and the Poles had already the support from the Polish nationalistic parties. Both sides tried to see their "outside power." German unification resulted in the strengthening of the fear of Poles living in Silesia and of the intolerant, nationalistic attitudes and actions.

Another, very recent example of the situation of minorities is a conflict between the Roman Catholics and the Uniates (Greek or Ukrainian Catholics) in Przemysl, in the south-eastern corner of Poland. Due to the obvious democratization of public life, the Uniates demanded that the Roman Catholic Church return the church buildings taken from the Uniate parishes soon after World War II. One of these church buildings used to be, during the inter-war period, the Uniate Cathedral. The Roman Catholic hierarchy that administered the church, decided to return it to the legitimate owners. Institutionally, not only in theory but also in practice, we have to do here with the recognition of the rights of cultural minority.

However, the public, collective behavior of members of the Roman Catholic Church was different. The parishioners decided to occupy the church building and called a hunger strike in protest to the action taken by their own Church hierarchy, which in their opinion betrayed them. They thought that Poland, including its churches, is solely for Poles and Roman Catholics. It did not matter to them that the building in question had been in the possession of the Uniate Church for several hundred years. The conflict lasted for weeks until eventually at the beginning of March 1991 most of the parishioners reluctantly decided to comply with the order of their church authorities.

In both cases, we have to do with the "demanding cultural minorities." Neither the demands nor the reaction on the part of the majority group was possible before the democratic transition.

Let us summarize these points and present some conclusions. The Communist system in Poland guaranteed neither majority nor minority rights. The democratization process in Poland, on the other hand, included the recognition of the need of the government to respond to the preferences of its citizens, which are taken to be equal politically. As a consequence nearly each individual and each group felt free and even obliged to express oneself on political and cultural matters without fear of governmental reprisal. However, the situation became complicated. The government found itself under pressure from two points of view. On the one hand, it met the demands of a majority which had been deprived for a long time by its cultural and political rights. It satisfy the needs of this group, it sometimes had to suppress the rights of certain minorities which were held responsible for the economic and political crisis. On the other hand, it felt obliged to respond positively to the demands of certain minorities which had also been suppressed culturally, political or both under the previous regime. The government tried to satisfy all these needs, with the exception of those of the unbelievers, which it considered to be outside the borders of Polish society.

The democratization process of the late 1980s and early 1990s did not involve granting everyone on Poland rights of citizenship but instead changing the scope of privileges. The minority that was privileged before lost its privileges, the majority of society gained privileges. Citizens who do not belong to the majority are actually deprived of many of their rights.

Robert Dahl's thesis that any political system is in peril if it becomes polarized into highly antagonistic groups and that subcultural pluralism often places a dangerous strain on the tolerance and mutual security required for a system of public contention turned out, in a sense, to be true in the Polish situation.

On the other hand, some additional observations should be made here. Poland's cultural minorities have been very small in number and therefore never dangerous for the cultural majority. Decades of socialization into intolerance resulted in a situation in which the demands for democracy actually meant demands for OUR full participation in public life, but not for everybody's participation. Demands for democratization meant demands for the right (meaning OUR) solution of problems but not necessarily demands for the right of public contestation of OUR decisions.

Dahl's thesis that subcultural pluralism places a strain on tolerance seems to be true, but the question arises if that is a very attractive thesis. What is the advantage of tolerance when we have no pluralism of preferences? Is it really pluralism or is it rather political or cultural monopolization that is dangerous? How can loyalty to a system of values that fostered the success of the democratization process be transformed into a tolerance that is crucial for democracy to function but inevitably means acceptance of the existence of values that are not OURS and have even been fought by us?

For the interpretation of the transition period in Poland (and, most probably, other East European post-Communist countries as well), Dahl's theory of democracy seems to be more useful than other theories of democracy but less useful that a sociological conflict theory. This general approach stresses the significance of group interests (economic, political and cultural) and power relations in different kinds of social conflicts, the results of which can change the groups' relative positions in the social structure. Sociological theory of social movements would also be useful in showing how structural conditions and available resources help some groups organize themselves and prevent other groups from doing so. And finally, cultural sociology would help analyze the situation of cultural minorities that have no structure or organization.

7

FROM A CONTROLLED MASS MEDIA SYSTEM TO A PLURALISTIC ONE

Henryk Galus
"Glos Wyzborcza" Newspaper, Gdansk

The transformation of a controlled mass media system into a pluralistic one constitutes an important element of post-totalitarian changes in the organization of the state and public life in Poland between 1989 and 1992. However, the progress made to date is assessed differently in political circles and in public opinion as well as by the users of mass media and the researchers.

Some of the people involved in mass media programming and some of the audience are of the opinion that the intended change has been now been thoroughly implemented and was faster than those changes taking place in other spheres of life. They also claim that this change in the mass media system constitutes a factor stimulating the overall social transformation. Political elites perceive this change in terms of their own options regarding programming and through the practical utility of press, radio and television with respect to realization of their political goals. Until now, there has been no systemic research conducted.

A sociological analysis of Poland's mass media system should encompass all forms of publicly available information, with the main focus being placed on the institutions devoted to information delivery and staffed by trained specialists. This involves a large number of institutions which can be grouped into ten categories:

1) press, radio and TV stations; 2) information agencies; 3)publishing companies and radio-television institutions together with promotional and advertising agencies; 4) printing houses; 5) distributors and broadcasters of radio and TV programs; 6) censorship agencies; 7) state and social authorities with administer press, radio and TV; 8) the legal structure regulating mass media; 9) colleges and other institutions which train journalists and deal in an academic way with social communication; 10) journalist organizations.

In order to show what transformations have occurred in the past three years and how the Polish mass media functions now, it is first imperative to give at least a bird's-eye view of the situation in the People's Republic of Poland (PRP) between 1945-1989.

1. Mass media within the structure of the PRP

Undoubtedly, the mass media of the PRP had all the features characteristic of totalitarian or authoritarian systems, even though the specific details varied in comparison with other communist bloc countries. Polish mass media was more open, flexible and professional than in other communist countries.

Elements of a pluralistic system of social communication certainly appeared in Poland during the first three years after World War Two as a result of a spontaneous rebirth of Polish press and radio following the years of German occupation. However, the foundations of a monopolistic and centralized information system run by one party possessing absolute power in the hands of the so-called "nomenklatura" in order to direct instruction and apply censorship were established at the end of the 1940s and early 1950s. The three pillars of the system date back to this period. The first is the Workers Editing Cooperative "Press, Book-Ruch" (PBR), a consortium of editing, reproduction and distribution services which had the status of a quasi-cooperative and the authority to monopolize nearly the entire range of press and journals. The other two pillars were institutions subordinated to the government but in fact controlled by the structure of the Communist Party: the Polish Press Agency (PPA), dating from 1945, and Radio-TV (RTV) Committee which developed out of the Central Radiophone Office founded in 1949.

These essential features survived up until 1989 in spite of some modifications in the function of the media and periods of temporary liberalization which proved necessary under pressure of social forces in certain periods of social crisis and conflict or through the efforts of journalists who, however, on the whole had no alternative but to perform their jobs within the party-state mass media system.

As a result of the events in October 1956, the most drastic deformities were removed, i.e. deep isolation from the world, primitive and aggressive propaganda and the identification of the mass media with the authorities. Other essential features of the system remained intact practically until the end of the PRP. Those features are: 1) control over all mass media from one central power; 2) involvement of the "nomenklatura" in personnel policies; 3) accreditation of journalists according to ideological and political criteria in times of crisis and the increase of totalitarian tensions (1948, 1968, 1982); 4) toleration of certain press activities alongside of the PBR, with strictly limited access to paper, limited print run and distribution; limitation of the flow of external information (jamming of foreign broadcasts in Polish was stopped by 1980 but permits for satellite antennas were introduced).

Nevertheless, the entire powerful mass media system did not function uniformly in terms of its particular aspects even in periods of relative stabilization, to say nothing of periods of crisis and conflict. The mass media revealed the different orientations of the party, the authority centers and the spontaneous demands of the society. It is not possible to ignore the role of some members of the press and editorial staffs in softening the monopolistic system of power and stimulating changes in periods of breakthrough. The role of the media for those circles was to 1) inform the society more exhaustively and objectively; 2) ease censorship and other limitations regarding the press and its role in presenting various political and ideological convictions; 3) acquire permission to publish new titles or send broadcasts for those involved in these circles.

In spite of the fact that the controlled system of mass media was shaken as late as August 1980, the time arrived for demanding a social character of the press, radio and television, pluralism of information, limitation of censorship and the legal regulation of the functioning of the mass media. This was fulfilled, and the independent "Solidarity" press is indeed a remarkable achievement on a large scale.

The August protests and the first period of "Solidarity's" legal activity were regarded by a large part of the professional journalists as a good moment to remove many illnesses in the monopolistic system and to establish a journalism which would properly inform society with honest information and enable a free presentation of opinions.

The martial law was lasted from December 13, 1981 until July 22, 1983 brought about a suspension of nearly all the press and a dissolution of an association which encompassed nearly all of Poland's journalists. Such an event had not occurred in Europe since the end of World War

Two. It was reinstated however after those journalists were banned who did not agree to work under the conditions imposed by martial law. This operation involved the banning of thousands of journalists and the "pacification!" of about ten-thousand others. Between 1982 and 1983, the system was built up and continued to function even between 1984 and 1988.

The journalists who were expelled from work entered the so-called "second circle" of press and publishing, the first step toward a pluralization of the mass media in Poland after the Round Table contract was reached in March and April 1989 and Solidarity was victorious in the parliamentary elections in June.

2. Transformations between 1989-1992

The Round-Table agreement brought small tactical gains to the Solidarity-opposition group because it acquired a daily and several journals, radio and TV programs and an overall liberalization of censorship. The opening of even small independent information channels secured an election victory for Solidarity. The next step of ending limitations to publishing activity and to control of paper opened up the way to free activity which was finally freed after the abolition of censorship in March 1990. The fight for the mass media between Solidarity and the former structures of power began in Autumn 1989.

The first non-Communist government under Prime Minister Tadeusz Mazowiecki implemented an information policy which tried to take control of the main centers of information coordination, the large state connected institutions such as RTV, PPA and the government daily "Rzeczpospolita". This partly based on the principle that "obedient will stay obedient." Changes in the staff were limited to the most essential, i.e. to the people who had lost public credibility. The journalists who wanted to come back after the rejection in the previous regime were subjected to bureaucratic procedures, which resulted in many disappointments. The changes in TV and radio and in PPA were rather superficial. While the leadership changed, the staff, which had established habits and connections with the former power elites, did not.

The pluralistic tendencies were readily noticeable in the daily press. Alongside of the press colossus PPA a new free "Solidarity" as well as other parties and factions in opposition began publishing activities. The strength of that trend was mainly reflected by the popularity of "Gazeta Wyborcza", which become the most widely sold newspaper in Poland. Significant role was also played by "Tygodnik Solidarność" (Solidarity Weekly) and "Solidarność- Tygodnik Gdański".

The political diversification of Solidarity which began in Spring 1990 under the slogan "war at the top" with the rivalry of Lech Walesa and Tadeusz Mazowiecki during the presidential election led certain newspapers and radio-TV stations to identify with specific political factions.

As an outcome of the rivalry, "Gazeta Wyborcza" lost its character as "Solidarity" paper and became aligned with the Democratic Union after the presidential election.

Financial, organizational and staff difficulties for the publishing at the beginning of 1990 caused a greater interest to develop in taking over those titles from the dissolved PPA which had been successful and financially sound. However, the bill decreeing the dissolvement of PPA in March 1990 the pluralization and privatization of the press was not specified clearly enough. It supplied two possibilities: the first enabled the transfer of titles to cooperatives, leading to an "affranchisement of the old and new press nomenklatura", the second involved the possibility of auctioning newspapers off to new editors by an office. This office was subject to various pressures.

The presidential campaign of Summer 1990 led to the transformational process for the press, radio and TV being frozen for half a year. The maintenance of the status quo was in the best interest of several groups, including the post-communist groups which had some influence on papers, radio or TV stations which were about to be sold or privatized. Subsequently, the bill to free these institutions from governmental control and establish independent controls was blocked. The decision about the PPA newspapers was held up and the institution charged with is dissolvement took over temporary management.

The liberal government of Jan Krzysztof Bielecki announced a speed-up in the breakup of the PPA monopoly and RTV but it took until the first half of 1991 to finalize the nearly complete privatization. Further reforms of radio and television were, however, stymied by disputes over the bill in Parliament.

3. Pluralism, political independence and commercialization

Television and radio are still under the control of the government of Prime Minister Jan Olszewski and his centro-right wing coalition in Parliament. The transformation into public media is dependent upon approval of the appropriate bill. This delay caused the emergence of broadcasting studios which had no formal permission. The variety of programs available is growing as more and more satellite and local cable television stations are established.

The situation of the daily press after the sale of the PPA titles remains unstable and changeable. There are twelve newspapers with a nation-wide circulation. With a half-a-million copies, "Gazeta Wyborcza", which represents the opinions of the Democratic Union, dominates the market. The new generation of newspapers indicate a pluralistic situation existing in competitive conditions, but it is too early to give a detailed assessment of their market positions.

Among the 56 regional dailies, there are only 19 new titles which have been established between 1982 and 1992 by private publishers. The rest have developed out of PPA. They rarely exceed printings of 100,000 and are under the influence of a number of political parties and groups. The situation of local TV and radio stations is quite similar.

The Church shows great expansiveness toward the mass media, not only the central and regional radio-TV stations, but also the print media. There is a Catholic daily newspaper with nation-wide circulation and a Catholic Society of Journalists.

There have been a number of changes in the range and scope of the print media. Both socio-political weeklies connected with the "Solidarity" movement as well as those associated with the former system have had a drop in readership. Surprisingly, the sol-called gutter papers are quite popular and the tradition women-oriented magazines have high circulation figures, along with new magazines devoted to issues of personal life and housekeeping.

The daily and weekly press and also the radio and TV news programs generally avoid clear identification with concrete political groups. They try to meet the criteria of objective information but differ in selection of material and commentaries. The political activity of the mass media during the presidential and parliamentary election campaigns was followed by a significant retreat from political issues, in particular in the regional press which must struggle to maintain a sufficient readership. As result there is an attempt to satisfy reader's interests and obtain paid advertisements. This creates a vicious circle because these aspects are expanded at the expense of general information, editorials and serious reporting, the lack of which tends to drive readers away.

The activities of journalist associations has dropped off and their position with publishers grown weaker. This constitutes new barriers for the freedom of press as an autonomous force in public life.

All of these matters point out new areas where research and broader study is needed.

PART IV

MARKET ECONOMY AND SOCIAL SOLIDARITY

8

THE POLES' ATTITUDES TOWARDS PRIVATIZATION

Janusz Erenc and Krzysztof Wszeborowski
Department of Sociology, University of Gdansk

Young democracies in Central and Eastern European countries are faced with serious problems. Established upon fragile formal structures, they do not reflect the real configuration of power between the various social groups. The character of the political turning point in 1989/1990 determined changes which involve actions of authority (using various state instruments) and (much weaker) process of building the bases for citizens' action. New political (central) elites are trying to modernize the state, but their actions are met with insufficient local activity and weak institutions of self-government. Thus it appears that the Polish society is fighting with various remnants of the old order, but not able to support new democratic tendencies. This is evident, for example, in the relationship of our society to the privatization of national property.

In this paper we would like to present some conclusions from the results of our two projects: "'Solidarity' toward ownership transformation", written for the Solidarity trade union and "On the privatization of shops and the premises of service", written for the Institute of Market Economy Research. We will also refer to some results of the research project "Poland and Poles" by the Institute of Sociology at the Jagiellonian University in Kraków.

More than 47% of the interviewees in our research for the Solidarity trade union said that they are fearful and even frightened of privatization. Nevertheless, every fourth interviewee said that privatization brings hope because it can improve the Polish economy and consequently better conditions of life. According to the research "Poland and Poles," 21.5% of those interviewed were convinced that they would like to work in private firms and nearly 50% said they liked working in public (state-run) firms. This result is rather surprising because at the same time more than half of our population (56%) were convinced that many private firms were necessary in order to achieve economic progress in our country.

This set of answers may seem paradoxical, but on the other hand are understandable. After World War II, the Polish economy was based on public firms. They created not only our economic but also social system. Now the transformation of this system needs not only new legal and organizing regulations but also, perhaps first of all, thoroughgoing changes in mentality. We should remember that during the last 45 years, i.e. over two generations, every Pole, from primary school upwards, was taught that public firms are best for the Polish economy. Thus, it is understandable that the famous works like Max Weber's "Economy and Society" has never been translated into Polish. The power of argumentation, when repeated systematically, and also the fear of unemployment (steadily increasing) commend people to be careful and discourages them from taking risks. The former Communist system guaranteed social security not only to good employees but also to bad ones, provided they were politically or socially engaged in the system. The sole supporters of families were also protected. According to our research, the great majority of our society still holds the policy of full employment as a major value, and subsequently think that the government should be responsible for its realization.

Unfortunately, it is apparent (and clearly supported in our research findings) that the designers of a new economic deal (system)--especially the creators of liberal conceptions--devote too little attention to these questions. The factor of social consciousness (mentality) is not taken sufficiently into account in these conceptions, and operational plans are not discussed adequately. As a matter of fact, the quick realization of the reform programs appears impossible. Of course, it should not be forgotten that one of the substantial variables which effects the image of the privatization process is the political system's instability. There is a lack of explicit programming and a lack of continuity in efforts of the successive governments.

The general evaluation of the present policy of ownership transformation is fairly low. Only one in every eight respondent thinks that the main direction of the present political and economic trends is correct. And, even among them there are some who object to the present policy of ownership transformation.

Among those factors which lead to a negative evaluation of the present policy, the most frequent one is the objection that particular social groups and strata (classes) of society are not treated in the same way. Some of those interviewed believe that privatization in the present form supports the post-Communist rules (nomenclature) and/or some groups of "crafty fellows" (smugglers, black market traders, etc.) who became rich during the Communist system more or less in collaboration with Communist officials. Recent Polish governments--especially the government led by the liberals--are accused of not controlling the process of ownership transformation, which resulted in many former directors and Communist party officials appropriating considerable material goods or profits. In our research interviews, people often described this as stealing of national property or selling "for a song" the state-run factories which had previously been made or declared bankrupt. They affirmed that prominent former officials still have considerable influence in certain regions as well as plenty of money, enabling them to buy (at little cost) the property of some public firms and organize their own private one.

The lack of an adequate or correct policy of information and promotion is another objection raised against the present governments. The citizenry expects comprehensive information about possible alternatives for the various firms and feels rather embarrassed when the consequent actions of new officials is not evident. In the opinion of the majority of people interviewed, the present form of privatization is a thoroughly chaotic process without any organizational framework.

There is also a lack of experts who are competent enough to direct the privatization process in some regions of Poland. Thus, the present attempt of radical transformation of the Polish economy resembles an attempt to build a skyscraper on swampy ground with a group of people gathered by coincidence.

The results of our research markedly show that there is no social approval for radical action in this connection. Only 12.2% of the respondents of the study "Poland and Poles" and 17% of the workers in the "Solidarity" study are ready to support rapid changes, i.e. a transformation of ownership relations via revolution. 80% of those interviewed declared they prefer privatization via evolution or a long-term process in which firms of all types of ownership (state, public or private) would have the same opportunities. The majority does not support the policy of protecting private firms but rather a scenario in which step-by-step reforms are implemented which do not lower the overall standard of living. The changes should be slow but effective, and above all, able to preserve the economic balance. Radical changes are connected with too great a risk which society cannot afford to take.

On the other hand, those interviewed criticize the indolence and slow pace of change. Poland was once a leader in the process of transformation within the East European bloc and now we are being outdistanced by others. This slowness not only damages many firms and causes them to lose the value, but also contributes to a decline in social engagement. Some believe that as the process of privatization becomes longer and the political situation more instable, people will lose faith that this way of solving our economic problems is proper. This is supported by our findings regarding the readiness of persons to buy shares in a firm (especially the firm where he or she works). In 1990, 74% of the Solidarity members replied positively, but last year the rate was only 58%, i.e. 16% lower than in 1990.

It may be asked to what extent the evaluation of the policy of privatization expresses the real relationship of our society to the process of privatization as a change in the economic system or to what text it is only an extrapolation. It may be that some political and social problems are attributed to privatization as people try to identify a cause for the lack of balance they feel. Privatization can be readily seen as a sign of change and thus become a target of criticism and a focal point for social dissatisfaction. It may be assumed that a considerable portion of the Polish people connect the present economic recession with incompetent policies by the present central and local governments, with the lack of a clear plan for solving economic problems and for organizing the process of privatization.

One of the pivotal questions related to the process of changing ownership is how workers can buy shares in state firms. Given the real conditions in our country--and probably in most other post-Communist countries--it is not only a technical and legal problem, but also a technical and legal problem. It should be solved with a measure of social justice, but this is often taken to be a "collectivistic" way.

It appears that the idea of common distribution of ownership-bonds which can be freely changed into shares of firms being privatized is the most preferred way of acquiring shares (39%). Considerable less support was given to other alternatives. Disposal of shares by selling them at lower prices was favored by 26%, by selling a convenient credit rates by 15%, and, least popular was the idea of selling them at full price (less than 3%). These results clearly correspond with the (often repeated) opinions about the rights of workers to the property of the firms where they work.

In answer to the question about the percentage of shares which should be distributed among the workers of a firm, nearly half of the respondents in the "Solidarity" study replied that the workers should have more than 51% of these shares. This solution would give them the possibility to take part in all the important decisions of their firms. This was especially supported by uneducated persons working in relatively small firms. Nearly one-fourth of the respondents favored a 33% rate of worker participation and a publicly proposed "network" of leading firms. About the same number of respondents supported a 20% rate of participation, the solution guaranteed by the privatization decree of the Polish parliament. It is worth noticing that the willingness to choose the latter solution increases correspondingly with the range of education of the respondent. Very few of the respondents were prepared to relinquish the privileges associated with owning shares. Taking this into account, it can be concluded that the guarantee of privileges can be a means of ensuring support for the process of ownership transformation. Of course, this does not mean that this is the way to win full acceptance for privatization attempts.

The results of our researches cited here show in general that there is a tendency to combine some market concepts with some "collectivistic" ideas. It supports the impression that the attitudes in Poland are still formed more by the old criticized system than by a clear idea of a new free-market based economy. Some people would like to achieve the aims associated with real socialism with institutions characteristic of the capitalistic world, i.e. integrating the principles of both of these social and economic systems (for instance, high efficiency of production and the policy of full employment). Perhaps the idea of a "new social and economic deal" can be seen as an attempt to find a "third way." It would be a combination of beautiful dreams and hard economic reality.

9

FROM REPRESSIVE TOLERANCE TO OPPRESSIVE FREEDOM: POLISH FAMILY FARMS IN TRANSITION

Krzysztof Gorlach and Zygmunt Serega
Institute of Sociology, Jagiellonian University, Kraców

W e would like to discuss here some basic elements of the transition process taking place on family farms in Poland during the change from a Communist system to one based on a market economy and political democracy. Poland has 2.1 million farms and more than 20% of its total labor force is involved in the private agricultural sector. Bearing in mind that individual farmers are in fact the only major class who saved their independent economic basis in the Communist system and formed one of the most important social groups challenging Communist power (Lane Kolankiewicz 1973), it might be said as well that this group has been a significant and effective political force. During the very hard period of Polish history after martial law was declared in December 1989, this political force succeeded in the struggle to defend its economic and political interests. In the first half of the 1980's the Communist authorities were forced to add to the constitution of the Polish People's Republic a clause to the effect that family ownership in agriculture should be treated equally with state and cooperative forms of ownership in the national economy.

However, in the post-Communist period (i.e. from summer 1989 when the first Solidarity-based government was formed) Polish farmers also organized some spectacular protests to defend their interests. There were several road blocks by tractors and farm machinery, a sit-in strike in the Ministry of Agriculture building in summer 1990, hunger strikes and protest marches in the streets of Warsaw in 1991. As a result of this, some people, including political commentators and even some sociologists (see Mokrzycki 1992) have started accusing farmers of being a force opposed to economic reforms in Poland.

Thus, there is a justifiable need for a careful analysis of family farming, in order to describe and explain the paradox that the most important and largest group of private owners in the Communist economy--where family farming was treated as a residue of a market economy--has become one of the most important forces calling for state intervention in the economy.

In trying to explain this problem, a two-fold strategy of reasoning can be followed. Firstly, one can point out some general phenomena occurring in the agriculture of various countries including the most advanced once with a long tradition of capitalist market economies. One will find that the activities of Polish farmers are quite similar to those of farmers in western Europe or in the United States. Demands for minimum price limits for agricultural commodities, subsidies for agricultural producers, food import limits, and the promotion of export of agricultural commodities are voiced by farmer organizations all over the world. Demonstrations, road blocks, strikes and the destruction of agricultural products to keep their prices from falling--such phenomena can be observed from time to time in many European Community countries. However, this aspect is not the main issue of our paper.

The second approach is based on the assumption that farmers, like other groups in Polish society, are burdened with the tradition, experience and patterns of behavior formed in and inherited from the Communist system. Some people express this thesis in an ideological sense by describing the typical Polish mentality as so-called "homo sovieticus." However, a more analytical approach to the problem requires a more detailed study. Some elements of such an approach may be found either in a sociological analysis dealing with the social awareness dilemmas of the transitional period (Sztompka 1991) or in considerations of the possibilities of and obstacles to the introduction of capitalism in Poland (Kochanowicz 1991).

We will use this second approach in our study and suggest a two-fold analysis. On the one hand, we will describe the family farming situation in the Communist system and in the transitional period. One the other hand, we will try to illustrate some elements of the strategies adopted by farmers in a typical rural community we studied in central Poland. This research was part of a broader research plan carried out among private farm owners in the second half of the 1980s in several regions of southern and central Poland. We investigated the problem of the relationship between the state and the private farming sector. The research was carried out in 1987 using interviews based on a questionnaire completed by 180 farmers (Gorlach and Serega 1991). In 1991 the fieldwork was repeated with further interviews of 174 farm owners.

1. Repressive tolerance and its consequences

The concept of "repressive tolerance" based on Herbert Marcuse's famous idea (Marcuse 1976) has become the framework used to describe the situation experienced by farmers under Communism. It shows, we believe, the nature of relations between peasants and the state in the above-mentioned time period (Gorlach 1989). On the one hand, these relations were based on elements of political and administrative repression towards peasant agriculture and attempts to subordinate this sector to the state-directed economy. On the other hand, some elements of tolerance can be observed, especially in the face of food shortages when peasant agriculture was the main source of agricultural commodities (Kuczynski 1981; Gorlach 1990). But the limits of tolerance were established by the Communist socio-economic and political doctrine which, despite official statements to the contrary, made evident the privileged position of the state and cooperative sector. This was revealed by the legal maximal limitations on acreage owned by individual farmers as well as the problems associated with buying new land.

In practice, during the Communist period the private economy was unable to integrate naturally with the state sector. However, because the direct elimination of family farms was unsuccessful (compare attempts at collectivization of peasant farms in the Stalinist period) some steps towards so-called artificial integration were taken (Banaszkiewicz 1988). As a result, family farming was subordinated to local state and political bureaucracy. Local state agencies ("urzedy gminne") created by the reform of the state administrative system in 1973 were obliged to control agricultural production on family farms. In many cases, they decided about the volume and type of commodity to be produced by particular farmers. This was especially true for specialized farms which were heavily dependent upon state credits and other supplies whose distribution was controlled by state agencies.

Local bureaucracy was also responsible for the land market, for instance, in deciding whether a private farmer would be allowed to buy land appropriated by state authorities when an old owner acquired a state pension. This bureaucracy also had the right to decide whether a farmer could buy, for instance, a tractor or any other heavy equipment at the state-controlled price. In other words, the opportunity to buy machinery at a reasonable price depended on the decision of the local bureaucracy. The farmer could, in fact, be forced to buy such goods on the so-called free-market at much higher prices.

Local state agencies controlled the system of agricultural services and local banks as well. They also ran the local system of so-called cooperative agencies which bought agricultural products from farmers and sold chemicals, pesticides and other supplies to them. The tax-collecting offices and farmers' advisory agencies were also a part of this system.

As a result it might be said that the entire range of farming activities took place within the framework controlled by the state authorities and became a peculiar game within the Communist system. It gave rise to a specific strategy among family farmers which can be called "a game for survival" within the Communist system, as represented in the first instance by the local state administration units. The essential aim of this game was to use the elements of tolerance in state policy to maintain family farming despite the elements of repression.

In addition to this general strategy, the repressive tolerance system gave rise to other characteristic elements of the family farmers' reasoning and activity. Some of the most important ones will be briefly discussed below.

The first issue deals with the amount of land possessed by the farmer. From the global perspective this a problem of the agrarian structure of peasant farming. The period of repressive tolerance prevented a concentration of farmland in peasant family farms at a level comparable to Western countries. For example, the average size of a family farm in Poland in 1989 was only 7.2 hectares and almost 70% of such farms were smaller than seven hectares (Rocznik Statystyczny 1990, 319-320).

Despite processes which might have caused farmland concentration, such as a mass migration of rural residents to urban areas beginning in the 1950s or demographic processes of generational change etc., structural changes have occurred slowly. This can be attributed mainly to the lack of real economic competition among agricultural producers (Adamski and Turski 1990). While some changes may be observed such as a slow increase in the number of farms of 10 or more hectares and in the percentage of total farmland cultivated by this kind of farm, no essential changes in this area have been visible since World War II (Szemberg 1991a, 1991b).

These phenomena are also reflected in the farmers' consciousness and the kind of production they tend to favor. Farmers used to think in terms of 5-10 hectare farms based on mixed farming principles. According to previous sociological research, the preferred farm acreage reflected in most cases the regional or even local situation (Adamski 1974, 189-192; Kocik 1986, 51). Farmers' experience in the past two years has not changed this type of reasoning. According to our own investigations in 1991, 56% of the farmers questioned pointed to the 6-8 hectare farm as the optimal model of a family farm, which is in fact a typical farm size in the community under investigation. Only 17% of the family farm owners declared that larger farms would be necessary in order to deal with the new situation.

Another issue deals with the mechanical equipment among farmers. Shortages in the market of agricultural machinery which were typical of the Communist economy led to certain characteristic pattern of thought. The most important phenomenon can be called the "psychosis of possession", whereby farmers want to have every available machine and agricultural equipment, even if it is not directly needed. This is a particular expression of the general attitude so typical of the "economy of shortages" in Communist systems.

In addition, this tendency was strengthened by the inefficiency and corruption of the state system of agricultural services. For example, during harvest time many farmers did not have access to agricultural services because of the shortage of equipment possessed by state agencies. Moreover, the bad quality of such services led farmers to prefer to own all the equipment they might need. Of course, in many cases, such technical self-sufficiency was irrational in view of the farm acreage or the level of its market orientation (Kocik and Serega 1985, 45-47, 78).

Nevertheless, this tendency is still present among farmers. More than 85% of our respondents in 1991 expressed the opinion that technical autonomy or self-sufficiency is still necessary today. Less than 10% of the respondents demonstrated rational thinking by stating that the amount of technical farm equipment should depend on the economic parameters of the farm (acreage, production profile, etc.) or that some forms of collective ownership can be quite useful for more sophisticated and expensive technical equipment (combines, heavy tractors, etc.). However, increasingly tougher economic and financial constraints are causing such collective types of ownership to be seen as a possible solution among our respondents. 30% of them were of the opinion that collective ownership would be required in the future. "Technical equipment for farmers becomes more and more expensive while farmers themselves have less and less money" stated one of the farmers interviewed.

It has been seen that this short period of experience within the new economic conditions could bring about some changes in the way of thinking about one's farm and its future. However, these changes have occurred in certain spheres of reasoning but not in others. Let us therefore try to analyze some of the effects of this new experience in more detail.

2. Oppressive freedom and the new experience

The period of political and economic reforms which began after the first Solidarity government was formed could be called one of "oppressive freedom." From the point of view of family farming, the most important change introduced in the economic and political doctrine was the elimination of limitations on private ownership. It was granted equal rights with other types of ownership in the national economy. Moreover, it might be said that is has even become the preferred type of ownership and widely regarded as an institutional pledge in the process of economic transformation towards the market system. In terms of agriculture, there are now no legal limitations on buying farm land or on a maximum farm acreage.

As to the relations between family farms and local administration units, it should be stressed that all the rules and systems of control have been abolished. Local administrative officers are no longer the decision makers who regulate the volume and type of commodity produced in administrative areas. This kind of state regulation of the economy has been replaced by market forces. On the global level, the role of the state has been limited to financial intervention (bank credits, interest rates, etc.) or of the buying up of agricultural commodities surplus (Agency of the Agricultural Market).

It can be said, then, that political constraints and administrative repression have been replaced by economic ones. This means that the market game and no longer the game with the local authorities is the main factor shaping the functioning of family farming and its future. At the same time, the introduction of market forces into the Polish economy has opened some new possibilities for other, previously unknown factors to reshape the reality of family farming.

Three such situations can be readily identified. Firstly, the influence of external factors when Polish agriculture, as well as the entire national economy, is put to the test by opening up to the European and world economic system. Secondly, some regional differences within Poland have started to operate in a more significant way than in the past. Large and commercial family farms in the northern and western parts of Poland have started to dominate over the small and traditional farms found mainly in central, eastern and southern areas. Thirdly, local features are beginning to play a role as neighboring farms with different levels of market orientation start to compete with each other.

As a result of the changes and factors mentioned above, the specific situation of "oppressive freedom" has emerged. It is characterized by a lack of political pressure and limitations imposed by the administrative system and the need for farmers to make their own decisions every single day and adapt to changing economic rules.

3. First experiences: the case of the farmers' community

Let us now compare some research findings from 1987 and 1991 in order to illustrate the effects of farmer's new experience. Using the example of a typical farmers' community, we will try to answer two basic questions:

a) how do the farmers under investigation see the essential problems faced by family farms?

b) what are the possibilities for activity in the new situation?

The answer to the first question is illustrated by farmers' opinions about the most significant difficulties in running a farm during the periods of "repressive tolerance" and "oppressive freedom". Their opinions demonstrate the level of recognition of the most important fields of constraint.

The views voiced form the basis for the thesis that the present situation of "oppressive freedom" is <u>more difficult</u> than the previous period of "repressive tolerance." Only 3% of the farm owners interviewed feel that they presently have no problems in running their farm. Four years ago 30% of the respondents gave this answer.

In addition, the difficulties experienced today are different from those experienced four years ago. Current pressures are mostly financial and connected with the comparatively low prices for agricultural products. Almost 80% of the answers mentioned this in 1991, while only 14% did so in 1987. The next frequently named difficulty was in selling agricultural products. This was mentioned in one-third of the answers of the most recent survey, while none did so four years earlier. The state administration system, on the other hand, was more frequently seen as a source of problems in the earlier period. In 1987, almost 8% of the respondents complained about its inefficiency and 13% complained about its restrictive policies and insufficient allocation of scarce products. Nowadays, these issues are entirely marginal in the minds of the farmers interviewed (2% and 5% respectively).

The next stage of our analysis of farmers' statements shows how they see the survival of their farms after their first experiences with "oppressive freedom." Almost half of the respondents revealed a strategy of unusual helplessness, stating that "nothing can be done." Almost 17% care willing to implement a strategy of pressuring the central government, which is regarded as responsible for the farming situation. Almost 15% of the respondents propose a strategy of increasing their own efforts. Three smaller groups of respondents propose introducing changes in their own economic activity. 6% feel that they need to take up additional work off the farm. Another 5% are of the opinion they should increase specialization on their farm. And 5% feel they should be prepared for a faster reaction to market forces by reducing the specialization on their farm and producing different types of commodities.

These research findings form the basis for the following empirical generalizations. Firstly, there is clear increase in the awareness of economic pressure with the result that prices, profitability and sales are the main issues being thought about. Secondly, there is a weakening of the tendency to see local authorities as a source of help in solving the problems and difficulties which are most basic to farming. Thirdly, a large percentage of farmers (almost half of the group we interviewed) has no idea about how to act in response to their first experiences with the system of "oppressive freedom."

4. Conclusion

In the face of the new experiences, two different strategies can be observed in the family farming community. The most widespread reaction among our respondents is a lack of any new plan of action and a simultaneous awareness of strong economic pressure on the farms and families. With the local administration no longer seen as a partner in the game for survival of the farms, this strategy can be seen as an attempt to transfer behavioral patterns developed on the local level to the global society. The fundamental problem, therefore, becomes the farmers' game for survival with the central government, which is seen as setting the rules. It is natural, therefore, that a large percentage of respondents point to certain general problems which the central authorities ought to solve for the farmers. The results of adopting such a strategy include an inclination to indulge in spectacular protest activities in an attempt to attract widespread attention to the oppression suffered by the farm families. This strategy can be described as an attempt to implement learned patterns of behavior (interaction with the authorities) while changing the focus of this behavior from local to central authorities.

The second strategy which is being implemented consists of changing patterns of behavior and playing a different kind of game, i.e. the market game. Belief in this strategy is expressed by opinions stating that changes must be introduced on farms, one's own efforts increased and certain economic cooperation undertaken between farm owners themselves (e.g., joint ownership of modern farm machinery). However, acceptance of this strategy makes the growth of competition between farms in a given community inevitable and, in the long run, will encourage more individual activity and the decay of communal ties.

Bibliography

ADAMSKI, W. (1974): "Chlopi i przyszlosc wsi. "Warsaw, Polish Scientific Publishers.

ADAMSKI, W. AND R. TURSKI (1990): "Interesy klasy chlopskiej jako zrodlo sytuacji kryzysowych." In: W. Adamski (ed.), Interesy i konflikt. Studia nad dynamika struktury spolecznej w Polsce. Wrockaw: Ossolineum.

BANASZKIEWICZ, B. (1988): "O stygmatyzacji i sztucznej integracji indywidualnej gospodarki rolnej w warunkach dominacji nakazowo-rozdzielczego systemu gospodarczego (na prrzykladzie rozwiazan prawno-ustrojowych)." In: J. Wilkin (ed.), Gospodarka chlopska w systemie gospodarki socjalistycznej. Warsaw: Warsaw University Press.

GORLACH, K. (1989): "On repressive tolerance: State and peasant farms in Poland." In: Sociologia Ruralis, XXVIII/1, pp. 23-33.

GORLACH, K. (1990): "Socjologia polska wobec kwestii chlopskiej."Cracow: Universitas.

GORLACH, K. and Z. SEREGA (1991): Chlopi we wspolczesnej Polsce: przedmiot czy podmiot procesow spolecznych. Cracow, Warsaw: Polish Scientific Publishers.

KOCHANOWICZ, J. (1991): "Is Poland unfit for capitalism?" Program on Central and Eastern Europe, Working Paper No. 10, Cambridge: Minda de Ginzburg Center for European Studies, Harvard University.

KOCIK, L. (1986): "Rodzina chlopska w procesie modernizacji wsi polskiej. "Cracow: Jagiellonian University Press.

KOCIK, L. and Z. SEREGA (1985): "Problemy funkcjonowania gospodarstw indywidualnych w warunkach wysokotowarowej produkcji rolnej,. "Opole: Silesian Institute Publishers.

KUCZYNSKI, W. (1981): "Po wielkim skoku." Warswa: Polish Economic Publishers.

LANE, D. and G. KOLANKIEWICZ (1973): "Social Groups in Polish Society. "London: MacMillan.

MARCUSE, H. (1976): "Repressive tolerance." In: P. Connerton (ed.), Critical Sociology. Selected Readings. Harmondsworth: Penguin Books, pp. 301-329.

MOKRZYCKI, E. (1992): "The legacy of real socialism. Group interests and the search for a new utopia." in W.D. Connor and P. Ploszajski (eds.), *Escape from Socialism: The Polish Route.* Warsaw: IFiS Publishers, pp. 269-282.

SZEMBERG, A. (1991a): "Zroznicowanie gospodarstw rolnych (tendencje w latach 80-tych). "Warsaw: Instytut Ekonomiki Rolnictwa i Gospodarki Zywnosciowej, zeszyt #300.

SZEMBERG, A. (1991b): "Prognoza przemian w strukturze obszarowej chlopskiego rolnictwa do roku 2010." Warswa: Instytut Ekonomiki Rolnictwa i Gospodarki Zywnosciowej, zeszyt #296.

SZTOMPKA, P. (1991): "Dilemmas of the great transition. A Tentative catalogue," Program on Central and Eastern Europe, Working Paper No. 19. Cambridge: Minde de Ginzburg Center for European Studies, Harvard University.

PART V

SOCIOLOGY AND SOCIETY IN POLAND TODAY

10

REVOLUTIONARY CHANGES AS A CHALLENGE FOR SOCIOLOGY

Jacques Coenen-Huther
Department of Sociology, University of Geneva

S ociological thinking started when the social order stopped being considered as a natural order, given by God, to be taken for granted, but rather as a construction of humankind, subject to variations in time and space.

For this reason the ancestry of sociology has quite commonly been traced back to the philosophy of Enlightenment in the 17th and 18th centuries. And indeed, the philosophers of the Enlightenment saw the individual as naturally rational, they were convinced that human reason had to be freed from traditional bonds. Only then would the social order become a matter of contract between free individuals, and the way would be open to progress.

But we all understand, or should have understood by now, that the ideas of the Enlightenment--for all their inspiring power--have often led to a very unsociological perspective on social life, neglecting the intermediate structures which are the backbone of society.[1] And the great classic works of sociology, written in the second half of the 19th century and at the beginning of this century, took shape partly in reaction to the

---

[1] See on this: Peter L. Berger (1977, pp. 167-180).

pre-revolutionary illusion of society as a collection of individuals, free from social pressures and the weight of traditions, guided by pure reason. Durkheim took great pains to emphasize the non-contractual elements of contract, Pareto promoted a cyclical view of history, Tönnnies could hardly conceal his nostalgia for medieval tradition, Max Weber was very receptive to the Nietzchean challenge to rationalism.

In fact, as the American historian of sociological tradition, Robert Nisbet, convincingly put it, there seems to be a Golden Age in sociology between 1830 and the turn of the century in which intellectual creativity was stimulated by the feeling of being torn between two worlds : the old world of feudality and tradition, the new world of democracy and capitalism.

It means that modern sociology developed out of a paradoxical two-step process. First, there was the growing awareness of the relativity of any social order. Second, there was a romantic reaction to the radical changes brought about by the Industrial Revolution and the French Revolution.

The 19th century reaction to large-scale social change can be understood as the product of the acute perception of a multiple crisis :

- crisis of the social bond, with the forms of sociability of modern society, or Gesellschaft, threatening the way of life of the old community, or Gemeinschaft.

- crisis of legitimacy, with naked power in competition with legitimate authority.

- crisis in social hierarchy, with an analysis in terms of status competing with an analysis in terms of classes.

- crisis in the world view, with the competition between religious beliefs and a secular view of the world.

- crisis in the understanding of history, with the very idea of progress challenged by a growing sense of alienation.

Now, it should be realized that when one starts speaking of a golden age, be it in philosophy, in arts or in science, it means that there is a feeling of uncertainty about further developments.

The idea of a golden age in sociology rests on two elements-- a clear transition between two social orders and an inner conflict of allegiance between two sets of values, the ones which are disappearing with the old way of life and the ones which are emerging out of the social change. If we follow this line of thought, there are reasons for uncertainty about the future of Western sociology. The transition has been completed. The revolutionary changes which started at the end of the 18th century have resulted, for better and for worse, in a new world which has little in common with the world that disappeared in the meantime. Will the works of our classics keep giving impetus to new lines of research and theory building ?

These were questions which were raised during the last decades in the West. To quote from Nisbet, in a book that was first published in 1966, "it ... becomes ever more difficult to squeeze creative juices out of the classic antitheses that, for a hundred years, have provided theoretical structure for sociology (...). It becomes ever more difficult to extract new essence, new hypothesis, new conclusion, from them. Distinctions become ever more tenuous, examples ever more repetitive, vital subject matter ever more elusive" (1966, 1980, p. 318).

In the meantime revolutionary changes began to take place in the last decade in central and eastern Europe where history had followed a different course. It is only at the end of 1989 that the magnitude of the change was fully perceived, but it is widely understood now that the crucial events of 1989 were the culmination of a process that had begun, roughly, ten years before.

And it can be said that in the post-totalitarian societies of central and eastern Europe, most of the people find themselves now torn between two worlds, just as strongly as may have been the case in the 19th century, with all the inner tensions related to such a situation. Is it a conflict between the relative stability provided by authoritarian regimes and the apparent chaos of emerging pluralism? Is it a conflict between the values of socialism and those of economic liberalism? In other words, is it a conflict between the experiments which have failed and the Western model, or is it much more than that?

Traveling in central and eastern Europe during the last years of the Communist regimes, the middle-aged Westerner had this strange feeling, at once very sad and charming, of making a journey into the past. Memories of the forties and the early fifties came to the fore. And of course, for very understandable reasons he usually refrained from saying so. He knew what he was standing for: freedom, the human rights, the end of oppressive regimes. But secretly in his heart he was hoping that some parts of a vanishing world would be preserved. Because they were parts of his own childhood. When he dug deeper into this "other Europe", the Westerner rediscovered forms of sociability to which he was no longer accustomed. A world he thought he had forgotten seemed to emerge out of the past : the world of his own grandparents. But those grandparents he met were no older than himself. Since the Westerner had seen the future already, he knew that the social life he rediscovered was bound to disappear soon with technological advance and economic improvement; in other words, with the liberation he was wishing for his fellow Europeans. So he used to return home with mixed feelings.

As for the people who made the opposite trip--those who somehow managed to escape to freedom--they saw the future, they became part of it, they realized that indeed it worked. But very often they were not so sure that they liked it, and grew ambivalent about the newly discovered reality.

And now that everything has been set in motion, everybody is understandably disoriented. The well-wishing Westerner knows that adaptation to the free market is a necessity. But he can hardly consider the advances of Western marketing practices as a victory for democracy. The expatriate who was able to provide significant help by sending a few dollars home, is anxiously watching the exchange rate of the zloty. The former dissident finds it increasingly difficult to identify friend and foe in a quickly changing political landscape. And those who just tried to survive in a system which froze society at an earlier stage of development are clearly at a loss in a new struggle for life, while the new rules of the game are still unclear.

Is this not exactly the kind of situation begging for a new Tocqueville, who is aware of the compelling necessity of drastic changes, but lucid enough to appreciate the damages done to the social fabric of society?

And indeed, the historical parallel with the revolutionary changes of the past might help us to a further understanding of current trends. The great founders of sociology were exposed to three kinds of ideological influences. First, the liberal view of the world which had shaken the traditional social order, Second, the millenialist dream of a radical change, purifying society of all evils once and for all. Third, a nostalgic longing for the medieval tradition dominated by aristocratic values.

Each of these currents of social thought has contributed to the sociological interpretation of reality, and it would be wrong to neglect one of them in defining the components of the sociological tradition.

Liberalism seemed to have exhausted its potential soon after the first World War. The secularised millenialism which had been a strong ingredient in a revolutionary tradition starting with the French Revolution and ending in the Bolshevik revolution of 1917 gave birth to the two totalitarianisms of our century.

These two totalitarianisms were powerful mixtures of utopian thinking and contempt for bourgeois liberalism and values. Both offered the prospect of a society purified of its alien elements and reaching an ideal stage: the classless society or the thousand-year German Reich. And the tragedy of Poland was that it was the victim of both of them.

If we turn to the Stalinist version of totalitarianism, imported here by the Soviet army, it should be pointed out that its filiation with some radical aspects of the French Revolution was-- and maybe still is-- particularly misleading. It were as if the philosophers of the Enlightenment had gone mad. Or maybe, just because of the pre-sociological character of their views, they were neglecting the organic character of society, over-confident in the power of voluntarism, forgetting the inescapable relationship between ends and means.

The dream of reaching universal justice through oppressive control had a strong appeal on honest men and women who were looking for a cause worth fighting for, and worth dying for. They saw themselves as the heroes of a time without heroes, and sometimes they were. Early activists were often people gradually led to intolerance, dogmatism, even fanaticism by a strong desire to stand above petty individual concerns. They were overwhelmed by a dream of belonging (Bauman, 1988), eager to find their way back to a lost community, subjugated by a charismatic leader. They became the Torquemadas of modern times, using and abusing power to bring about Utopia on earth at all costs, but finally when the grand social experiment proved to be a catastrophic nightmare, they were left as ONI, "they", the others ...

Should liberalism finally have won the century old ideological battle after all ? One could be tempted to think so. There is even at the moment the vision of an end of history in the form of a new world order based on the principles of democratic pluralism and market economy. And it looks indeed as if millions of people had only one desire: to live, as they say, "in a normal country", that is, like in the West.

But is liberalism really on the winning side? And is it to be identified with a democratic future? The least one can say is that many people in the East and in the West, for a variety of reasons, have doubts about it.

In the West, very few people are inclined to celebrate the collapse of the totalitarian empire of the East as a victory. We know all too well that the affluent Western society which developed in the mid-fifties is definitely not a product of liberalism; it is rather the product of an uneasy compromise between economic liberalism and social-democratic redistribution of resources. And it can even be said that this compromise was facilitated by a sense of menace in the East. The dynamic of market economy would not have developed so far without State intervention, State regulations and the protective network of welfare institutions. So, there is no such thing as a triumphant Western world looking upon itself as a model society. The West does not rejoice because the West has no recipe.

The apparent victory of liberalism in the West is based more on indifference, helplessness or disaffection than on positive support. Everything that has been achieved seems very fragile. Affluence seems to imply waste, freedom seems to imply alienation, social protection seems to imply unacceptable sacrifices. The three ideological currents of the 19th century are still there although in a different form. To be sure, the aristocratic values do not play any significant role anymore; they even have lost their meaning for most of the people. But the appeal of a mythical traditional world is widespread and certainly accounts for some of the discontents of modernity. As for the radical threat against the present social order, it does not seem to have vanished. There is the uneasy feeling that more unemployment, more immigrants in competition for jobs and housing, more efforts required to help the poor or the elderly could easily lead to some nasty resurgence of the most unpleasant past.

In view of this, the forced march of Poland towards market economy has something altogether admirable and frightening. Admirable, because once more we witness heroic determination, unbelievable endurance or the most ingenious arts of survival. Frightening, because after all the false promises of the past, people are requested once more to make sacrifices for a better future. In other words, they have once more to defer gratifications. And still, there is every reason to fear that dogmatic application of economic liberalism, based on a simplified view of Western societies, could very easily lead to the ugliest forms of exploitation. The more so since former communist cadres seem very eager to convert themselves into capitalist managers. One can only hope that there will be one more Polish miracle and that it will not turn into a mirage.

The foreign observer understands that the epic phase of the "longest Polish insurrection" [2] has come to an end. This means, and it is quite obvious, that the phase of political realignments has come. And the various collective actors involved might be haunted by the same ideological currents mentioned before. At the moment, I do not think that a playback of an earlier sequence of Polish history can be totally ruled out. After the rebirth of Poland at the end of the First World War, three models of society seemed clearly to be in competition for political power: the aristocratic model, the liberal-democratic model, and the revolutionary model. The aristocratic model was strong. The liberal-democratic model was weak. The importance of the revolutionary model had to be seen in relation to the geographical proximity of the center of World revolution and if it had not been for the "Miracle on the Wisla", the socialist experiment could have started in Poland at the beginning of the 1920s. In this context, the Pilsudski coup of May 1926, followed by the Sanacja regime, can be interpreted as an attempt to establish a specific

---

[2] I borrow this expression from Kazimierz Brandys (1981, 1985, p. 243).

synthesis of the three models (Davies, 1984). Back to present day Poland, it seems to me that the liberal-democratic view on society is still weak, in spite of the Polish orientation to the West. The revolutionary model is dead, but it does not mean that the millenialist dream of radical purification will not survive in another form; neither does it mean that the authoritarian style of government will disappear soon. An imprint has been left on people's attitudes. As for the aristocratic model, there is something which, in my view, deserves special attention. The aristocratic values, the ethos of nobility, seem more alive in modern Poland than in any other European country. This could be a very special feature of Polish society, partly to be explained by an element of social continuity from the 18th century nobility to the 20th century intelligentsia. According to Zygmunt Komorowski, "since the end of the 18th century", Polish intelligentsia has been formed as "a new and vigorous class... from the part of the nobility disinherited of their goods and offices after the partition of Poland".[3] And this special feature could set Poland apart from East and West, or rather to give it a specific position in between. In Russia, where the ruling class was living mentally in the pre-revolutionary 18th century till the revolution of 1917, aristocratic values seem to have been eradicated and are slowly dying in the second and third generations of the white emigration. In the Western world, dominated by the ethos of the middle-class, they have lost any real meaning .[4]

Beyond the political vicissitudes of the moment, the foreign observer is led to expect some kinds of long term realignments. At this stage, the paradoxical situations of the 1980s should be recalled:

- a government that was increasingly aware of the necessity of far- reaching reforms could no longer rely on its own political power basis to have them carried out. It had somehow to reach out to the forces of the opposition. And this finally led to the logic of the round-table. But it looks now as if a kind of dubious Wallenrod had been necessary to bring the process to maturation.

- a church which would have been considered as a force of political reaction everywhere in Western Europe, with the possible exception of Ireland, was in the vanguard of the battle for human rights.

- as for the opposition forces as a whole, they were a conglomerate of all possible shades of the political spectrum.

In a new geopolitical situation, the need for paradoxical alliances is quickly disappearing. What is left are the various conflicts of

---

[3]See on this: Zygmunt Komorowski (1974, pp. 185-186; 1981, p.5). See also: Janina Markiewicz-Lagneau (1982, pp. 54-55).

[4]The increasing obsolescence of the concept of honor is a case in point. See: Peter L. Berger (1974,pp. 83-96).

interests. We call them political issues and they are the ingredients of normal political life in a pluralistic society. But what are the <u>legitimate</u> interests in a country which is going through a period of revolutionary changes? This is also a question as old as the French Revolution and there is no easy answer to it. After the neo-Wallenrod will a neo-Pilsudski appear on the scene? Or rather a neo-Dmowski? In other words, will a kind of guided national consensus be necessary to muddle through, on the way to "normal life" ? Whatever the variant, such a solution carries an ominous threat. It entails the risk of a return to the rhetoric of exacerbated nationalism. From the Baltic to the Black Sea, romantic nationalism is making a powerful comeback. Of course, the concept of the nation-state in the nineteenth century romantic sense provided the best antidote against the destruction of cultural identity, foreign oppression and totalitarian aberrations. But it has already proven to be a regional risk as well. To be sure, as a result of all the cruelties of the forties, Poland has become culturally a much more homogeneous country than it was before the war. It means that problems of minorities will hopefully be easier to manage in a civilized way than in the 1930s. But a return to nationalistic politics would certainly poison the relations with neighbouring countries such as the Ukraine and Lithuania, to begin with. I very much hope I am wrong but it seems to me that it would not require too much demagoguery to induce some people to die for Wilno . [5]

What about sociology in all this? It seems to me that Polish sociology as a strong tradition of involvement in shaping policies. This was already clear after the foundation of the Polish Republic in 1918, when Znaniecki and other intellectuals of the Polish Diaspora came back home, and the various research institutes were founded (Markiewicz-Lagneau, 1982). This became apparent again in the mid-eighties, when sociological analysis led to a very courageous diagnosis of the state of Polish society which is still a source of inspiration at the moment. I refer, of course, to the work of the late Stefan Nowak, endorsed by the Board of the Polish Sociological Association (1988).

Sociological thinking is more relevant than ever in the present circumstances. And it seems to me that a systemic view on social reality is the best way to offer a modern translation of the organic character of society, pointing to the unintended consequences of purposive action. The present situation, for all its uncertainties and maybe because of them, is not only an occasion for social engineering. It offers opportunities for a whole program of general theory. Personally, I often use the Parsonian concept of social system, with its four sub-systems, as

---

[5]Several Polish colleagues assured me that on this point I am indeed wrong and that my fears are exagerated.

a convenient taxonomic tool. And it might be the place to remember that this structural-functional scheme was directly inspired by the work of another great figure of the Polish Diaspora: Bronislaw Malinowski.

If you keep in mind the four societal functions of the Malinowski/Parsons scheme (adaptation, definition of goals, integration, maintenance of the cultural pattern), you will realize that they all bring us to fundamental dilemmas and problems.

Adaptation, defining the sub-system of economy, translates at the moment into a clash of rationalities in this period of transition.

Goal-defining, or the political sub-system, requires the rise of a new political elite and the institutionalization of conflicts.

Integration, which is the product of the sub-system of social controls, requires the acceptance and enforcement of new norms of behaviour.

The maintenance of the cultural pattern requires clearly a new synthesis of values. And here we have come full circle. Indeed, it can be said that if such a synthesis between traditional and socialist values on the one hand, a spirit of enterprise on the other hand, cannot be found, the clash of rationalities will prevent the institutionalization of conflicts and will hamper the emergence of new norms of socially acceptable behaviour.

Now let us come back to the sociological tradition in an international perspective. After expressing scepticism about a sustained continuity in sociological creativity, Robert Nisbet suggested that new ways of conceptualizing social reality might emerge somewhere. And he wrote : "Perhaps it is taking place in our own day before our unseeing eyes, with some thus far mute, inglorious Weber or Durkheim even now encapsulating stray hypotheses and random observations into a new system for sociology" (1966, 1980, p. 318). For the reasons I have mentioned before, I would suggest that it is the confrontation of sociological consciousness with the social and political earthquake of central and eastern Europe which will make this possible, if it is possible at all.

Western sociologists should not come to Poland to teach or to preach, but to observe, to listen, to understand ... to try to understand.

Bibliography

BAUMAN, Janina (1988): *A Dream of Belonging. My Years in Postwar Poland.* London: Virago Press.

BERGER, P.L. (1977): *Facing up to Modernity. Excursions in Society, Politics and Religion.* (Paperback edition, Penguin, Harmondsworth, 1979).

BERGER, P.L., B. BERGER and H. KELLNER (1974): *The Homeless Mind. Modernization and Consciousness.* Paperback edition, Vintage Books, New York: Random House.

BRANDYS, K. (1985): Miesiace 1978-1981. French translation: *Carnets de Varsovie,* 1978-1981. Paris: Gallimard.

DAVIES, N. (1984): *Heart of Europe. A Short History of Poland.* Clarendon Press, Oxford. French translation: Histoire de la Pologne. Paris: Fayard, 1986.

KOMOROWSKI, Zygmunt (1974): *The Class of Intelligentsia in Africa.* In: Africana Bulletin, No 21, pp. 185-190.

KOMOROWSKI, Zygmunt (1981): *La religion et le sentiment religieux des Polonais.* Paper, Oran, Algeria, 13 p.

MARKIEWICZ-LAGNEAU, Janina (1982): *La formation d'une pensée sociologique. La société polonaise de l'entre-deux-guerres.* Editions de la Maison des Sciences de l'Homme, Paris.

NISBET, Robert A. (1966, 1980): *The Sociological Tradition.* London: Heinemann.

NOWAK, Stefan (1988): *Polish Society in the Second Half of the 1980s: An Attempt to Diagnose the State of Public Consciousness. A Statement of the Governing Board of the Polish Sociological Society.* Translated from Polish. Princeton: International Research and Exchange Board.

11

LESSONS OF POST-COMMUNIST TRANSITION FOR SOCIOLOGICAL THEORIES OF CHANGE

Piotr Sztompka
Institute of Sociology, Jagiellonian University, Cracow

One of the crucial features of the revolution of 1989 is its basically a-theoretical character. Normally, great revolutions have been preceded, and to some extent prepared by theoretical visions which provide legitimacy to the social forces which impel them, as well as to the goals being pursued. There were always some chosen groups or social classes considered as revolutionary agents (the "third estate" in the French revolution, the proletariat in the Russian revolution, the peasantry in the Chinese revolution). And there were always some, more or less utopian and always strongly normative images of a better society which the revolutions were intended to realize (as envisioned by the French philosophies, or Marxists, or Maoists).

Nothing of the sort was present in 1989. That revolution just happened, carried by a wide alliance of diverse social groups which cut across all traditional class, occupational, regional, or ethnic boundaries. It was inspired more by the repulsion against the existing system and an awareness of what was no longer acceptable, than by any clear notion of what was to take its place. It was not a revolution in the name of another utopia. It was not a revolution under the banner of ideology, but expressed rather disenchantment with any ideology. If there was anything resembling ideology at all, it consisted of those basic, almost common-sense values and precepts of classical Enlightenment and Western modernity, which were absent or at best feigned in the "life-world" of real socialism - such as truth and reason, liberty and dignity, individualism and self-realization, sovereignty and self-rule.

Thus it was not a revolution guided by any theory. It was also not predicted by any theory. Social scientists were hardly able to keep up with the developments of this revolutionary process, describing <u>ex post</u> and interpreting <u>ad hoc</u> each of the upswings, crises and downturns as they occurred, up to the final collapse of the communist system which took them all by surprise. Regrettably, there was little that the revolution could learn from the sociological theories of change. But perhaps the theories of change can learn from the historical experience of anti-Communist revolution and post-Communist transition? This is the question I wish to consider in the present paper.

For the sake of argument I will claim that the events of 1989 require a fundamental revision of the theories of social change, which have been around since the days of August Comte. Actually, to use an apt phrase of I. Wallerstein, there is a need not only for rethinking but "unthinking" of such theories (Wallerstein, 1991). The long 19th century, which in terms of social dynamics seems to have lasted almost until our day, is finally drawing to a close. A true paradigm shift is occurring. Paradoxically, the a-theoretical revolution is producing a revolution in theory.

There are four different levels at which one can discuss the theoretical implications of 1989: meta-theoretical, theoretical, empirical and heuristic. The meta-theoretical question deals with the logical status of the theories of social change, or the whole field of "social dynamics". Does the experience of anti-Communist revolution teach us anything about the viable forms of theorizing about change, the functions of theories in this area, their proper level of generality, their substantive scope? The second question is theoretical and has to do with alternative models, explanations or conceptual schemes put forward by the theorists of change. Which of those retain viability in view of recent historical events, and which have to be discarded? The third question is empirical and addresses the truth-value of particular theories when confronted with current historical evidence. Which of our cherished theories becomes falsified, and which of those abandoned earlier, perhaps a bit prematurely, seem to gain new supportive evidence and demand modifications in view of new facts? The fourth question is heuristic and seeks directives for future theorizing about change. Does the experience of the recent revolution tell us anything about the aspects, or problems which seem to present crucial challenges for the understanding of coming social changes. These four questions will be taken up in turn, and their sequence provides the logical skeleton of our argument.

1. The meta-theoretical question

Any theory worthy of its name usually gains recognition because of its predictive power. And at the same time, the most common complaint to be heard now among sociologists, or to be raised against sociologists by a wider public, is that no theory predicted the collapse of communism. The sociological theories of change were clearly not strong enough for that. It is the first lesson to be drawn: the lesson of modesty.

One interpretation of the predictive failure makes reference to epistemological limitations: the complexity of historical events of that scale, the lack of sufficient initial information, the lack of rigorous, mathematical models etc. All that of course can potentially be improved. But I would submit more radical, ontological arguments. It may just be that in this area prediction is not just hard, but principally impossible. First, because such historical events depend on actions taken by multitudes of individuals, they occur as aggregate effects of myriad of individual decisions, and human beings happen to be at least marginally erratic, capricious, and indeterminable in what they decide to do. Second, because the mobilization and coordination of revolutionary actions demands strong leaders, and the appearance of such leaders with sufficient talents, stature and charisma is to a large extent a secret of genetics. Third, because a phenomenon of revolution incorporates multiple processes: the growth of discontent and grievances, mobilization of the masses, reactions of the entrenched elites, pressures of external powers - to name but a few. Each of these may be regular, theoretically accountable and to some extent even predictable. But in their concrete, unique combination, cross cutting a certain historical moment, those processes produce an irreducible novelty, a phenomena not explainable nor predictable by any partial theories. Fourth, because in the case of revolutionary social changes the circular logic of reflexivity and self-destroying prophecy is particularly vicious. By assuming, namely, that a theory is predictive, the prediction of revolution would certainly be acted upon by the defenders of the old regime, who at that moment would still have enough force to paralyze the revolution and prevent its victory, thus falsifying the prediction by their actions. Hence, a theory of revolution is impossible: either it is false, or it is not a theory at all.

I think we have to reconcile ourselves to the fact that in the area of large scale social changes we use the term theory in a much more loose sense than in the natural sciences. We certainly have to part with the positivistic notion of a theory, with its claim of symmetry between explanation and prediction. In speaking about theories of social change we have in mind a very generalized, abstract discourse aimed at providing intellectual orientation in the chaos of events and an <u>ex post</u> interpretation of historical events, rather than their rigorous explanation and prediction. It does not allow us to tell what will happen, but if it is any good at all, it gives some idea of what is happening, and which future scenarios are possible, which options are feasible and which can be excluded. It closes the field of possibilities, but never leaves only one, single option. It narrows down the area of uncertainty, but it never provides certainty. There is no reason to be ashamed of that; this in itself is a great feat. But there is also no reason to pretend that we have a truly predictive, rigorous theory, when this is in principle unattainable.

At which level of generality should one search for regularities of social change? It is a misleading shorthand to speak of the theories of social change, because social change as such does not exist. What does exist is the multitude of processes, concrete, causally linked sequences of events in various areas of social life: political, economic, cultural and psychological, macro and micro, at the level of individual biographies, group developments, national histories, global trends etc. Social dynamics should attempt to grasp the mechanisms and forms of such concrete processes. Viable theories of social change must not over generalize, but rather stay at the middle level of generality. Any real help in understanding and interpreting the events of 1989 comes from such middle-range theories (Merton, 1948)--of social movements, of relative deprivation, of collective behavior, of legitimation of interests, of interest groups etc.--rather than from grand historiosophical schemes addressing change as such. The second meta-theoretical lesson to be drawn is the lesson of concreteness.

Should theories of social change be conceived as universal, applicable to all societies and all epochs, or rather localized and time-bound, restricted in space to certain regions, cultural areas, political blocks, or even single nation-states, and limited in time, to certain historical periods? This question is independent from the earlier one. Both highly general and middle-range theories may be treated as universal, but valid only at some places and some times. Even a cursory glance at the course of anti-Communist revolutions in various countries of the former socialist bloc, and even more so at the processes of post-Communist transition, suggests the uniqueness of national experiences.

Compare Poland with Bulgaria, Czechoslovakia with Romania, Hungary with Russia, all of them with the former GDR. Differences seem to overshadow similarities. Valid theorizing cannot overlook them. It must seek the reasons of variety--in national traditions, geopolitical location, ethnic diversification, levels of economic advancement, education of elites, personalities of leaders--rather than sweep all these factors under the rug of some abstract theory of uniform transition. Similarly, valid theorizing must recognize the timing of processes, both in the relative sense of "before-and-after", as it is not irrelevant where the revolution started first, and where it only followed, which countries were earlier, and which later; and in the absolute sense of dating, as the whole historical configurations of 1980, or 1989, or 1992 are remarkably different, and hence different fields of possibilities were open (or closed) in those years. In short, the logic of processes must be grasped in the unique historical contexts in which they occur. This is the third meta-theoretical lesson: the lesson of uniqueness.

2. The theoretical question

In the almost two centuries of its intellectual history, sociology has produced a great number of theoretical accounts dealing with social change. But if we look beneath their actual variety and seek underlying commonalities, four images or models of social dynamics will be unraveled. The first is evolutionary (to be found in A. Comte, H. Spencer, and E. Durkheim among others), rooted in the metaphor of organic growth. It assumes gradual unfolding of social processes in a specific direction, toward some final state, moved by immanent (endogenous) potentialities. The process is seen as pre-determined, irreversible, and most often progressive, leading to the betterment of society.

The second model is dialectical (to be found in K. Marx and later Marxists). It retains the assumptions of determinism, directionality, irreversability, and finalism but adds three modifications; it describes the path of the process as step-functions leading through certain qualitative thresholds (social revolutions), it specifies the immanent potentiality as constantly re-appearing contradictions, strains and tensions (social conflicts), and it considers progressiveness only as the ultimate trend, realizing itself through regressions and crises (at the cost of a temporary growth in poverty, exploitation, alienation).

What is common to both models--evolutionary and dialectic-- is the belief that social change occurs in a necessary, irreversible, directional mode, somehow above the heads of concrete, acting individuals. They share the assumptions of determinism, finalism and fatalism. Common terms for both have been devised by their critics: K.

Popper's "historicism" (Popper, 1957), or R. Nisbet's "developmentalism" (Nisbet, 1970).

There is a third model (to be found in O. Spengler, V. Pareto, P. Sorokin and others), rooted in the metaphor of the wheel. This is the cyclical model. The assumptions of directionality, irreversibility, finalism and progressivism are suspended--there are repetitions, replications of the same phases, returns to the same states of society, no real improvement of human condition. But cycles are still believed to be pre-determined, necessary and asserting themselves in spite of any concrete actions people may take. Cyclical processes are seen as fatalistic and deterministic.

A radical break with determinism, fatalism and finalism-- and thus with all three earlier models of change--comes only in the last decade within two influential orientations: theories of agency, and historical sociology. The new image founded on the belief in a human creative and constructive potential, may be called the model of social becoming (Sztompka, 1991a). It considers social processes as contingent products of aggregated individual actions, taking in the conditions inherited from earlier actions. Or in other words, as the constant production and reproduction of society by human actors (Giddens, 1978).

Returning from this topological excursion to our main topic, I will claim that the experience of anti-Communist revolutions and post-Communist transition deals the last fatal blow to all varieties of historicism, developmentalism or determinist-cyclical models of social becoming.

First of all, no version of the Laws of History, as opposed to contingent laws of specific historical events, or Laws Concerning History (Mandelbaum, 1966), seems to hold any more. The present situation in the former USSR or Eastern and Central European societies fits into neither evolutionary, nor dialectical, nor cyclical schemes. It is far from any structural-functional differentiation or adaptive upgrading, which would be expected by the evolutionists (Parsons, 1975); it is certainly not unfolding toward Communism, to the dismay of the Marxists; and it seems without historical precedent, breaking rather than continuing the vicious cycles of reforms and backlashes, thaws and freezes, accompanying the whole history of "real socialism."

Second, the idea of Historical Necessity cannot be supported any more. The role of contingent events, chance, individual decisions and choices has been reaffirmed time and again (Elster, 1989). And likewise the obvious fact that at any historical moment, the number of open historical possibilities is much larger than one. Would the "Solidarity" movement have consolidated itself so quickly in August 1980, if Walesa had not joined the striking workers and assumed leadership? Would the movement have won in Poland in 1989, if Jaruzelski had not introduced martial law eight years earlier, supposedly to prevent Soviet military intervention? Would the Prague street crowds have kept to the limits of the "velvet revolution" if Havel had not decided to go "na Hrad"? Would the USSR have finally disintegrated if Yeltsin had not climbed that tank in front of the Moscow parliament at the hour of the putsch? Would the "autumn of nations 1989" have been possible at all, if Gorbachev had not abandoned the Brezhnev Doctrine and publicly announced that the Red Army would not intervene in the defense of an external empire? All those are, luckily, counterfactual questions. But any mental experiments will show that those actors and those acts were centrally important to the course and ultimate fate of revolutionary processes. And there was no necessity in their conduct. They could easily have been absent from the scene, and even if present they certainly could have acted otherwise. We have mentioned famous leaders because they are more salient and of course more consequential in their decisions, but the same applies to millions of common people and their choices, individually less consequential, but in the aggregate fully decisive. Each of them could also have acted otherwise. There is nothing that is pre-determined in history, because history is only what people make of it, by means of their actions.

Third, we have to part with the idea of the immanent Goal of History, some inescapable final point toward which history supposedly is moving. Social processes are not pulled by some ultimate, single end, rather they are pushed by innumerable actions and decisions of human individuals, acting on their visions, moved by varying and often conflicting images of desired goals. In the revolutions of 1989 they were moved by the simple, primordial desire of a better life, epitomized in the more or less idealized pictures of Western developed democracies. The Goal of History which is claimed by the Marxists to reside in Communism has not come about because ultimately almost nobody wanted it to. Does it mean that the liberal-democratic polity and market-capitalist economy provide the alternative "end of history", as the conservative apologists led by F. Fukuyama (1992) seem to assert? The spreading disenchantment with modernity, liberalism and consumerism, becoming a fad in the Western world at the close of this century, and expressed in the career of various post-modern, post-industrial, post-historical creeds and projects proves otherwise. People are always restlessly searching for a better world and, alas, never find what they were dreaming of. For the time being, the fetishes of the free market and parliamentary democracy seem to rule the imagination of post-Communist societies, but it is hardly the end of their history. What forms of social life will emerge from the present chaos is an entirely open issue.

Fourth, the idea of perpetual Historical Progress seems to be more doubtful than ever before. Not only because the closed, but prolonged historical episode of "real socialism" has shown how under the banner of progress, actual regress, misery and suffering can be procured for huge segments of human society. After all, this was not the first case of this sort in history, and could still be countered by some claims of long-range progress, supposedly proven by the very collapse of Communism (and similar earlier projects). But the real trouble is the identification of what counts for progress in present society. Look at the surprising, and steadily growing percentages of those who declare that their life conditions in fact deteriorated with the fall of Communism. But even if we discount such data as subjective, and look for objective indicators, the ambivalence of any criteria becomes obvious. Is it progressive to have full shops but lower wages, to bring down inflation but raise unemployment, to open free markets but limit local production, to give power to a democratic parliament but make the country ungovernable, to liberalize law enforcement but suffer upsurges of crime, to abolish censorship and witness the flood of pornography and third-rate literature? I mention just some of the current dilemmas appearing in the aftermath of the revolution in my own country. Experiences in other countries of the region would certainly sustain the feeling expressed in the title of the recent article by Vaclav Havel: Paradise is lost *again* (Havel, 1992). There is no absolute progress, but only relative and variable admixtures of progress and regress, of betterment and deterioration of human condition; and our judgment always has to depend on two questions: progress of what, and progress for whom? History moves back and forth, no Law of Progress holds, and no ultimate, universal blueprint for progress can be found.

All this adds up to our next lesson, no longer meta-theoretical but properly theoretical-the rejection of historicism and developmentalism. The reverse, positive side of the same negative message is the support we discover in the events of 1989 for opposite types of theory. Namely those which emphasize contingency of historical process; those which stress creativeness and constructive capacities of human agents, both Great Heroes and Common People; those which focus on concrete, situational and historical circumstances which shape the field of historical possibilities open to human choices; those which abandon the search for absolute and universal criteria of progress, and instead treat as progressive such societies which manifest viable agency - the potentiality of striving for their own self-transformation and improvement. Those are the themes brought together in contemporary theories of agency and so-called "historical sociology". Referring to the synthesizing statement of this position which I have proposed recently (Sztompka, 1991a), I would claim that the experience of the anti-Communist revolution suggests the viability of the theory of social becoming.

3. The empirical question

General theoretical models cannot be immediately and directly tested against empirical evidence in order to prove their truth or falsity. They can only be confronted with general contours of ongoing processes and be shown more or less viable and fruitful. This was our procedure in the preceding discussion. But there are also numerous conceptions within the field of social dynamics which take the form of specific, empirical theories and make direct claims about social facts. These may be subjected to verification or falsification. Let us see how some of them fare in view of the recent historical breakthroughs.

There are four theories of this sort which must be examined: modernization theory, convergence theory, dependency theory and the theory of world system. All of them are the products of post-World War II period. They have achieved the peak of influence in the 1960s and 1970s. Recent events have brought them back into the mainstream of sociological debates. It seems that they demand rethinking and revision, but with that proviso may still be helpful in understanding current historical changes.

All of them had a similar rationale: they intended to provide some understanding of the post-war social, political and economic order, with its pronounced division into at least three "worlds": the developed industrial societies, including Western Europe and the US, but soon joined by Japan and other "newly industrialized countries" of the Far East; then, the socialist bloc dominated by the Soviet Union and moving, at a huge social cost, along the path of planned, centralized industrialization; and finally there were the post-colonial societies of the South and East, severely underdeveloped and often remaining entrenched in the pre-industrial era. How to conceptualize and explain social change in such a heterogeneous, and clearly unequal global setting, taking into account growing mutual interdependence of the First, the Second and the Third Worlds? In the present paper, constrained by limitations of space, I will discuss only one of four major theories, perhaps best elaborated of them all, namely modernization theory.

The classical modernization theory was primarily concerned with the Third World and the ways to pull it up to the level of advanced model countries ("Reference societies", "pace setters") by purposeful transplantation of Western institutional patterns. The policy of conscious emulation, undertaken in planned ways by local governments, was advocated as the road to modernity. There were strong evolutionary overtones to the theory: it believed the process must be gradual, directional, unilinear and finalistic (catching up with tangible, existing examples of developed industrial societies) and its main mechanism was thought to resemble organic growth: proceeding via structural and functional differentiation and adaptive upgrading.

Strongly criticized on factual, theoretical and ethical grounds, the theory of modernization was abandoned in the 1970s. But already in the 1980s we observe signs of its revival (Tiryakian, 1985) and after 1989 it clearly finds a new focus in the effort of post-Communist societies to "enter, or re-enter Europe", as the phrase goes. The projects of "neo-modernization theory" (Tiryakian, 1992) or "post-modernization theory" (Alexander, 1991) are put forward. The revived and revised modernization theory takes into account the experience of the post-Communist world, and in effect modifies its central assumptions.

The crucial difference between modernizing processes in the Third World and in the post-Communist Second World is due to the legacy of "real socialism." Whereas in the post-colonial countries, the starting point was usually the traditional, pre-modern society, preserved in more or less unchanged shape, in the Soviet Union and Eastern Europe, both the ruling ideology and the highly politicized, centralized and planned economic system were for many decades involved in the promotion of modernization. But as a result, what has been achieved is far away from genuine modernity. It may be called "fake modernity". What I mean by fake modernity is the incoherent, disharmonious, internally contradictory combination of imposed modernity in some domains of social life, coupled with the vestiges of traditional, pre-modern society in many others.

Let us draw a simplified balance sheet of the legacy of so-called real socialism in this area. On the side of modernity, there was: imposed industrialization, with obsessive emphasis on heavy industry (remember Lenin's maxim: "Socialism equals electrification"), a shift from the agricultural to the industrial sector; extensive proletarianization; chaotic urbanization; highly efficient control of the population by a bureaucratic apparatus of administration, police and army; a strong autocratic state. There also appeared, sometimes in extreme degrees the unintended side-effects of modernity including environmental destruction, pollution, depletion of resources, anomie and apathy of the mass society. And what was missing, and is still absent these days was: private ownership; rational, accountable, calculable organization of production; the functioning market; the rule of law;

abundance of consumer goods and options; dependable "abstract systems" like telecommunication, airline systems, road networks, banking infrastructure (Giddens, 1990); robust entrepreneurial elites and middle classes; rooted work ethics and individualism; a functioning democratic regime. Somehow, perversely, these societies seem to have attained all the dreary sides of modernity, and shunned all its bright sides. They have paid the costs, without reaping the profits. This strange and schizoid legacy is still around, and is probably there to stay for a generation or more.

But it is not only that Eastern Europe has inherited fake modernity, in some respects it also returned to a pre-modernity lingering all those decades under the facade of the unified socialist bloc. Internally - autocratic regimes, and externally - the imperial domination, have suppressed all primordial divisions, producing fake homogeneity and consensus. Ethnic, regional, religious diversity disappeared for the time being. With the fall of the external empire and ongoing internal liberalization, well-suppressed but never outgrown pre-modern loyalties, solidarities and attachments had to reappear. The bloc as a whole, and each country internally, emerged more divided and internally split that anybody could have predicted, as if frozen in pre-modern era with all its national, ethnic, regional conflicts and resentments. The unifying effects of capitalism, the market and democracy did not operate, and once the artificial blockades were lifted, the pre-modern, ugly face of Soviet and Eastern European societies appeared in full clarity. All this requires serious rethinking of the concept of modernity and the theories of modernization. Such an effort is already in process and its directions can be grasped by means of ten points.

First, the agency, the driving force of modernization is no longer seen as restricted to governments, or political elites acting "from above." Rather, the mass mobilization "from below" on behalf of modernization, most often contesting the inert or conservative governments, becomes the focus of attention. Spontaneous social movements and emerging charismatic leaders, are considered to be the main modernizing agencies.

Second, modernization is no longer seen as a solution devised and accepted by enlightened elites and imposed upon resistant, traditionally-oriented populations, as was most often the case in the Third World countries. Rather it reflects commonly held, spontaneous aspirations of the population, inflamed by the demonstration effect of Western affluence, liberty and modern life-styles ("Dynasty syndrome"), as perceived through the widely available mass-media or personal contacts.

Third, instead of the emphasis on endogenous, immanent forces of modernization, the role of exogenous factors is recognized, including the world geo-political balance, the availability of external economic and financial support, the openness of the international markets, and last but not least, the availability of convincing ideological resources: political or social doctrines or theories encouraging modernizing efforts by affirming the values of modernity (e.g. individualism, discipline, work-ethic, self-reliance, responsibility, reason, science, progress, freedom).

Fourth, in place of the single, unique model of modernity to be emulated by backward societies (in classical theory, most often the model of the US), the idea of "moving epicenters of modernity" is introduced, and its corollary, the notion of alternative "reference societies" (Tiryakian, 1985). It is claimed that the American model may not necessarily be relevant for post-Communist societies, and that in general the Western pattern of modernization is not necessarily superior, exportable and applicable everywhere. The suggestion that Japan or "Asian Tigers" (NIC's) are more relevant examples, appears more and more often.

Fifth, in place of a uniform process of modernization, a more diversified image is proposed. It is indicated that in various areas of social life modernization has a different tempo, rhythm and sequence, and in effect desynchronisation of modernizing efforts is apt to recur. R. Dahrendorf warns against the "dilemma of three clocks" which is facing post-Communist societies and argues that in the area of legal, constitutional reform six months may be enough. But in the economic domain, six years may be too little. And at the level of deep-lying life-ways, attitudes, and values making up the modern "civil society", its renewal may take generations (Dahrendorf, 1990).

Sixth, a less optimistic picture of modernization is drawn, avoiding the naive voluntarism of some early theories. The experience of post-Communist societies clearly shows that not all is possible and attainable, and not all depends on sheer political will. Much more emphasis is put on blockades, barriers, "friction" (Etzioni 1992; Sztompka 1992), and also inevitable reversals, backlashes and breakdowns of modernization.

Seventh, instead of an almost exclusive concern with economic growth, much more attention is directed toward human values, attitudes, symbolic meanings, and cultural codes, or in short--"intangibles and imponderables" (Sztompka, 1991b), as pre-requisites of successful modernization. The classical notion of "modern personality" is revived, but given a different role; it is no longer treated as the desired outcome of modernizing processes, but rather as a necessary precondition for economic take-off.

Eight, the anti-traditionalist bias of the early theory is corrected by pointing out that indigenous traditions may hide important pro-modernization themes. Instead of rejecting tradition, which may be counterproductive by provoking strong resistance, it is rather suggested to exploit tradition, by discovering "traditions of modernization", and treating them as the legitimation for current modernizing efforts. This may be particularly relevant in the case of former socialist societies, which before the long episode of "fake modernity", which actually froze them in the pre-modern state, usually had experienced some periods of capitalist growth, or democratic evolution (e.g. Czechoslovakia or Poland between World Wars).

Ninth, the internally split character of post-Communist societies, with some enclaves of modernity resulting from imposed industrialization and urbanization, and extensive lacunae of pre-modernity (in widespread attitudes, life-ways, political institutions, class composition etc.), opens up a central issue of strategy: what to do with those tangible vestiges of real socialism, e.g. the huge state-owned, and most often technologically outdated industrial enterprises? The main debate revolves around the proponents of the Big Bang" approach (Sachs, Aslund, Balcerowicz), advocating complete deconstruction of the economic, political and cultural remnants of socialism, i.e. starting modernization from scratch; and the "gradualists" who would like to salvage existing heritage, even at the cost of slower advancement toward modernity. As the arguments of both sides are convincing, the resolution of this issue remains open.

Tenth, and the last factor which makes the present modernizing efforts of post-Communist societies certainly different, and perhaps more difficult than the modernization of Third World countries after World War II, is the ideological climate prevailing in the "model societies" of the developed West. At the end of the 20th century, the era of "triumphant modernity" with its prosperity, optimism, and expansionist drive seems to be over. The crisis, rather than progress, becomes the leitmotif of social consciousness (Holton, 1990). Acute awareness of the side-effects and unintended "boomerang effects" of modernity produces disenchantment, disillusionment and outright rejection. At the theoretical level, "Post-Modernism" becomes the fashion of the day. It seems as if the Western societies were ready to jump off the train of modernity, bored with the journey, just at the moment when the post-Communist East frantically tries to get on board. In this situation, it is harder to find unambiguous ideological support for modernizing efforts, running under the aegis of liberal-democracy and market-economy, which is the only conceivable direction, if we discount the fascist alternative, and some misty and mysterious "Third Way". The generalized account of this peculiar predicament has to find its place within a revised modernization theory.

The example of modernization theory demonstrates how historical events may provide powerful stimuli for rethinking, reworking and fundamentally revising those sociological theories of change which have direct empirical relevance. Other theories of this sort listed at the beginning of this chapter--convergence theory, dependency theory, and world system theory-- are undergoing similar revisions. Their consideration, though, would require another paper.

4. The heuristic question

Now I would like to tackle briefly the remaining heuristic question: what major substantive emphases, problematic areas, and focal issues may be suggested for future theorizing about social change, if we take into account recent historical experiences of post-Communist societies? This will provide a tentative agenda for a new, more adequate theory.

The first area, which has clearly been of extreme importance in the process of overthrowing of communism, and seems even more central in the course of post-Communist transition, has to do with psychological and cultural factors, or more precisely, with mentalities and rules. Compared to the economic and political aspects, those are clearly under-explored and under-theorized. This is because we are dealing with the realm of intangibles and imponderables, hard to grasp in a precise way, and even harder to pinpoint with empirical tools. But these epistemological or methodological difficulties should not mislead us into believing that such facts are not real in a hard ontological sense or that they are unable to exert strong causal influence on more tangible domains of thoughts and actions. It is indeed striking how commonly sociologists of quite diverse theoretical persuasions intuitively affirm their presence and significance. Consider the variety of terms, some of them characteristically metaphorical, used with reference to such intangibles and imponderables. The best known are those old and somewhat discredited notions of "national character" or "modal personality." But there are others. R. Bellah borrows an idiom from Alexis de Tocqueville in speaking of the "habits of the heart" (Bellah, 1985); R. Dahrendorf of the "frames of mind" (Dahrendorf, 1990); B. Seebacher-Brandt of "the imponderables of the soul of the people" (quoted in Dahrendorf 1990), E. Morin of "l'esprit du temps" (1965). Terms like "social climate," "social atmosphere," "social mood," "the soul of society," "the public mind," "the public morale" have entered the vernacular. The sociologists coming closest to our own focus and reflecting on contemporary situation in post-Communist countries speak of "psychological and socio-moral infrastructure of collective life" (Lutynski, 1991) and "social subconsciousness" (Marody, 1987). And recently, social theorists proposed a specialized technical vocabulary: "cultural biases" (Thompson, Ellis, Wildavsky, 1989). "habitus" (Bourdieu, 1990), "discourses" (Alexander, 1990). I believe that incorporation of such intangibles and imponderables into rigorous sociological theories is the most pressing challenge for the future. It may be called the lesson against one-sided materialism or economism. The second area, centrally important but insufficiently researched, has to do with historical tradition. One of the most surprising discoveries of post-Communist changes is the persistence of tradition, of the "burden of history" (Jedlicki, 1990). Both in the sense of the immediate legacy of "real socialism" which manifests tremendous resistance to reform, and in the sense of an earlier historical heritage, which was seemingly absent for several decades, reappears immediately once the paralyzing grip of autocratic polity and imperial domination is released. Here the case of revived nationalisms, regionalisms, religious allegiances is particularly telling. What is the sociological mechanism of such long-range transmission of tradition, across many generations, under the most unconducive circumstances? This is an urgent question to be put on the theoretical agenda. Recent history teaches us a persuasive lesson against presentism.

The third area covers the actions of great individuals, of charismatic leaders, but also of the common people, who in their masses produce aggregated historical effects. It is high time to bring people back into the theories of change. But what are the mechanisms of recruitment, selection, socialization of outstanding individuals, who are then able to leave such a tremendous imprint on historical processes? How do they reach the positions and roles allowing them to become eventful and event making (Hook, 1955)? And how do the minute actions of common people, taken for their own private reasons and idiosyncratic purposes, sometimes add together to change human history? And how do common people sometimes actually get together to fight for new shape of society? In spite of the irresistible intuition that both Great Heroes and Collective Action were decisive factors in the course of recent transformations, we don't have much systematic knowledge about that. It implies a call for more research in this direction, and it also provides a lesson against mechanicism and collectivism.

The fourth area demanding vigorous research is the globalization of social processes in contemporary world. The inter-dependence of events--economic, political, cultural--on a scale far outreaching the borders of nation-states, regions, political blocks, or even continents, radically changes the context of every historical change, and significantly modifies its course. We know perfectly well that what was happening at the Kremlin and at the White House, on Wall Street and the Tokyo Stock Exchange, in the Middle East and Afghanistan, in the Vatican and the Sacred City of Khom proved to be vitally relevant for the collapse of "real socialism". But how those international, global flows of determinants and influences really operate remains to a large degree a mystery. We also do not know much about the social mechanisms of those spreading "infections"--of cravings for freedom, democracy, individual dignity, embracing within a short time vast areas of the globe; or of those waves of social movements (Tarrow 1990) mobilized for the same cause in distant lands, only to return to passive acquiescence some time later. The phenomenon of "the Autumn of Nations 1989" turns our attention to this new world-wide scale of social processes. And it provides our last important lesson against provincialism.

This is the brief, but theoretically very profuse agenda for the sociology of change.

5. Conclusion

But, one may ask, is a new, more adequate theory of change, utilizing the lessons of anti-Communist revolution and post-Communist transition, really needed? Who cares about theory expect frustrated theorists, whose predictions somehow never come true?

I believe that the common people do. And if they don't, they should. Because great social upheavals leave them uprooted, without guidance, devoid of orientation. It is precisely the aim of sociological theory, in the sense advocated in this paper, to provide such orientation, introduce order into the chaos of new experiences, give meaning to the avalanche of events, eliminate anomie in this special sense of the term.

In periods of fundamental social changes, the need for theories of change has always been acutely felt. Is it by accident that the first wave of sociological theories of change came in the 19th century in response to the birth of modernity, the great transition from traditional, to modern industrial society? And is it far-fetched to expect that the second wave of sociological theories of change may follow this rebirth of modern society, occurring in radically different circumstances at the end of the 20th century - the great transition from fake modernity to genuine modernity within the former Communist empire? Such theories may become one of the important factors upon which the success of present transition will ultimately depend.

Bibliography

ALEXANDER, J.C. (1990): "Democracy and Civil Society", Los Angeles, UCLA. Manuscript, 125 pp.

ALEXANDER, J.C. (1991): "Post-modernization theory", Los Angeles, UCLA. Manuscript

BELLAH, R. (1985): "Habits of the Heart." Berkeley: University of California Press.

BOURDIEU, P. (1990): In Other Words. Cambridge: Polity Press.

DAHRENDORF, R. (1990): "Reflections on the Revolution in Europe." London: Chatto & Windus.

ELSTER, J. (1989): "Solomonic Judgements. "Cambridge: Cambridge University Press.

ETZIONI, A. (1991): "A socio-economic perspective on friction," Washington: IAREP/SASE Conference. Mimeographed

FUKUYAMA, F. (1992): "The End of History and the Last Man. "New York, Free Press.

GIDDENS, A. (1990): "The Consequences of Modernity. "Cambridge: Polity Press.

HAVEL, V. (1992): "Paradise Lost." In: The New York Review of Books, April 9.

HOLTON, R. (1990): "Crisis and Progress." In: J. Alexander and P. Sztompka (eds.), Rethinking Progress. London, New York: Unwin & Hyman.

HOOK, S. (1955): "The Hero in History. " Boston: Beacon Press.

JEDLICKI, J. (1990): "The revolution of 1989: the unbearable burden of history,'"in: *Problems of Communism,* July-August, pp.39-45.

LUTYNSKI, J. (1990): "Nauka i polskie problemy: komentarz socjologa, " (Science and Polish problems: The Sociologist's Comment). Warszawa: State Editorial Institute.

MANDELBAUM, M. (1966): "Societal Laws," in: W.H.Dray (ed.), *Philosophical Analysis and History.* New York: Harper & Row, pp. 330-346.

MARODY, M. (1987): "Antynomie zbiorowej podswiadomosci" ('Antinomies of collective subconscious'). in: Studia Socjologiczne, No. 2, pp. 89.

MERTON, R.K. (1948): "The Position of Sociological Theory," American Sociological Review, vol.13 No. 2, pp. 164-168.

NORIN, E. (1965): "Duch czasu, "Krakow, Znak Publishers.

NISBET, R.A. (1970): "Developmentalism: A Critical Analysis," in:McKinney, J.C. and Tiryakian, E.A. (eds.), *Theoretical Sociology*, New York: Appleton Century Crofts, pp. 167-204.

PARSONS, T. (1975): Societies: Evolutionary Perspective, Englewood Cliffs, Prentice Hall.

POPPER, K.R. (1957): "The Poverty of Historicism," London: Routledge & Kegan Paul.

SZTOMPKA, P. (1991a): "Society in Action: The Theory of Social Becoming," Cambridge: Polity Press and Chicago: Chicago University Press.

SZTOMPKA, P. (1991b): "The Intangibles and Imponderables of the Transition to Democracy", in: *Studies in Comparative Communism*, Vol. XXIV, No.3, pp. 295-311.

SZTOMPKA, P. (1992): "Dilemmas of the Great Transition", Cambridge, Mass.: Harvard University, Minda de Ginzburg Center for European Studies (occasional papers series).

TARROW, S. (1990): "Aiming at a moving target: social science and the recent rebellions in Eastern Europe" Minneapolis: The University of Minnesota. Mimeographed.

THOMPSON, M., ELLIS, R., WILDAVSKY, A. (1989): "Cultural Theory."
Berkeley. Pre-publication manuscript.

TIRYAKIAN, E. (1985): "The Changing Centers of Modernity", in: E.
Cohen, M. Lissak, U. Almogor (eds.), *Comparative Social Dynamics*.
Boulder: Westview Press, pp. 131-147.

TIRYAKIAN, E. (1991): "Modernization: Exhumetur in Pace", in:
International Sociology, No. 3, June.

WALLERSTEIN, I. (1991): *Unthinking Social Science: The Limits of
Nineteenth-Century Paradigms*. Cambridge: Polity Press.

12

POLISH SOCIOLOGY IN A TIME OF RESTRUCTURATION

Antoni Sułek
Institute of Sociology, University of Warsaw

P oland is undergoing a systemic transformation as one system, the Communist one, rapidly collapses, and another one slowly emerges. Because this is happening in a country in which sociology has been well developed for a long time, it is possible for the links between sociology and the changing system to be observed. This is an opportunity seldom granted to sociologists, since, in general, sociology is developed in developed countries, and these do not have to change their systems.

The relationship between the change taking place in the system and sociology is not, in Poland, a unidirectional one, since it is reasonable to wonder about the role which sociologists played in shaping the new consciousness of society, in the social movements which led to the change of system, and maybe even in the political processes which have followed the collapse of Communist rule. However, these problems don't interest me here. Moreover, generalizations regarding this subject would have a conspicuously impressional character and would--

according to the principles of cognitive psychology--[1] certainly overestimate the significance and positive role (by today's standards) of sociologists in the change of the system. In contrast, my task is to describe the influence of the transformation on sociology and to show how sociology has reacted to the systemic change.

The term "sociology" conceals various aspects of one and the same discipline. Firstly, sociology is sociologists themselves, the sociological community, or, as Robert Merton says,[2] the sociological tribe. Sociology is also sociological practice, the sum of the professional activities of sociologists. Above all, however, sociology is the product of these activities, i.e. the notions, facts and generalizations which sociologists have arrived at in striving to understand society. However, although this last aspect is the most important, it will not concern me, as these products of sociology are included in all of the Polish papers presented at this seminar.[3] I am left with the first two aspects.

I will thus speak about the influence of the systemic change in Poland on the community of sociologists and on sociological practice. More precisely, I will show how a great social change changes also the conditions for sociology, and the way in which it is carried out. It creates new areas of study, opens up new possibilities for research, creates new roles for sociologists and promotes new methods of research. I will also present some results of the systemic change which have been unexpected and--for sociological interests--unfavourable to the discipline. This paper is not based on any systematic survey, but on participant observation of the sociological community and on readings of its production. And the standpoint from which I observe sociology will certainly have influenced the results.

1. New areas for empirical research

"May you live in interesting times!" - this wish has come true also for sociologists. There is hardly another generation of Polish

---

[1] See A. G. Greenwald, The Totalitarian Ego. Fabrication and Revision of Personal History, *American Psychologist* 1980, Vol. 35 No. 7, pp. 603-618.

[2] R. K. Merton, Remarks on becoming honorand of Jagiellonian University: Social Time and Socio-Cognitive Networks, *International Sociology* 1990 Vol. 5 No. 1.

[3] Let alone the books devoted entirely to the transformation, both in English and Polish. The most recent are: S. Gomulka, A.K. Polonsky (eds.) Polish Paradoxes, London: Routledge 1991; W.D. Connor, P Płoszajski (eds.) Escape from Socialism. The Polish Routes, Warsaw: IfiS Press 1992: J.R. Wedel (ed.) The unplanned Society. Poland During After Communism, New York: Columbia University Press 1992; M. Marody (ed.) Co nam zostało z tych lat... Społeczeństwo polskie u progu zmiany systemowej. Londyn: Aneks 1991; J. Mucha et al. (ed.) Spoleczeństow polskie u progu przmian, Wroclaw: Ossolineum 1991; A. Sulek, W. Wincławski (ed.) Przełom i wyzwanie. Pamietnik VIII Ogólnopolskiego Zjazdu Socjologicznego, Warsaw: Polish Sociological Association - Torun: Nicolaus Copernicus University 1991.

sociologists which has lived in times as interesting as these. One process as fascinating as today's breakdown of Communism was its establishment immediately after the Second World War, but studies of that process have only recently begun, primarily by historians and not sociologists. At that time of its origin the number of sociologists was small and they did not have the freedom to study it. Another process as extensive and as profound as the current one was the imposed industrialization beginning in the early 1950s. Research into its social aspects became a passion of sociologists, but only after the restitution of sociology. i.e. in the second half of the 1950s, when industrialization was already in progress. In contrast, it has been possible for sociologists to follow the breakdown of the Communist system from the very beginning.

For many years Polish sociologists disclosed facts at variance with the official vision of society and processes, which were for them at first only pathologies of the existing structures, and later already the processes of disintegration of real socialism. The mass protest of 1980 and the formation of Solidarity was as much a surprise to them as to everybody else (including the leaders of the protest). However, in the 1980s they argued convincingly that social conflict had in no way died out, but was merely frozen, that the authorities had lost their legitimacy and that the crises was continuing as a result of the failure to adjust political and economic structures to the needs of society. Furthermore, sociological thinking in the 1980s had reached a theoretical level, i.e. sociologists were able to describe relations between the "society" and "the system" in a subtle way, and to uncover the mechanisms stabilizing the system and the tensions within it which accelerated the disintegration and change of the system.

For Polish sociologists, systemic change has become a fascinating field for observation and empirical study. It is quite obvious that their interest has focused upon various aspects of the departure from the monocentric political system and the command economy, and the transition to--what is believed to be--a civil society, political democracy and market economy. Therefore, popular subjects of study have become elections; the creation of political parties; the development of the private sector in the economy; changes in the job market, particularly unemployment; changes in the functions of religion; and the changes in social consciousness, particularly in the public opinion that accompanied all these changes.

When taken as a whole, sociological research on the transformation has two characteristic features:

1. As recently as one or two years ago, almost everything that Polish sociologists studied was interpreted in terms of the "transition from totalitarianism to democracy" (TTD). However, critics of sociology

were rather quick to point out that such a perspective is in part a priori and expresses collective "wishful thinking"; that, in other words, Poland is not simply a place where some historic pattern manifests itself, some necessity, which will lead inevitably to the appearance of the market and democracy of the Western type. In addition, the transformation in both the political and economic spheres, to say nothing of the thinking of society, has turned out to be considerably slower and more difficult than had been anticipated; in Poland it has clearly lost its initial dynamism.

These circumstances have modified the priority areas of research in an interesting way. Having seen how difficult change is, sociologists are turning their attention to factors favorable to continuity in order to show how cultural traditions and group interests shaped in the period of real socialism and the mentality formed at that time interact with the new economic and political mechanisms. It is also worth noting that the numerous problems, which undoubtedly are the problems of the period of "transition", are being studied without any explicit reference to this "transition", let alone by locating them along a "totalitarianism - democracy" axis. These references are sometimes superfluous because they are obvious, but sometimes, because they are poorly defined, they contribute little and would play only an ornamental role, instead of relating a particular problem with a general theory.

2. A descriptive, idiographic approach is dominant in empirical studies of the transformation period. Sociologists are simply trying to record unique processes which are happening before their eyes. An awareness of the historical character of these changes and the need to document them is common to all. It is certain that when historians study our times they will draw widely from sociological research, just as the historians studying the People's Republic of Poland drew on studies into industrialization or changes in social structure.

In these studies, the theoretical perspective is rarely present. There should at least be more use made of general sociological description, as for example in electoral studies. The routine registration of electoral behavior, the establishment of the socio-demographic conditioning of elections and the study of electoral trends is of interest to many Polish sociologists, but rarely do they use the results of their electoral surveys as indicators of deeper orientations and social processes (in the West, electoral studies are not even necessarily included in sociology; they have a separate name - psephology).

Let us hope that this lack of balance between the development of empirical studies and of theoretical thinking is only a matter of time and the lack of a satisfactory quantity of empirical material for the construction of generalizations. Let us recall, however, that the absence of an empirical (not to be confused with normative!) theory of socialism was explained for such a long time by reference to its "young age" and that sociological theories of the system of real socialism did not appear until the system itself had begun to go into decline!

2. New possibilities for study

The systemic change in Poland not only created new areas of study for sociology but also removed, or considerably weakened, the political barriers to social studies.

1. The most obvious influence of the democratic changes on sociology is the considerable reduction in the range of subjects which are politically taboo. As censorship of questionnaires was lifted, the state stopped forcing researchers to take into account the views of the state regarding what and how they were and were not allowed to ask. State institutions have also become more easily accessible to penetration by researchers. The study of local power at the level of local community was allowed in the 1960s, the study of regional power elite was allowed in the 1970s, and now even the study of members of parliament is permitted. This example shows that the widening of the freedom to make social studies had an evolutionary character and the real socialism was a system which allowed itself to be studied quite well - even by opposition-minded sociologists!

Paradoxically, the decentralization and pluralization of public life in Poland is a source of some problems that were previously unknown. For example, there is no authority which will order a state enterprise, let alone a private one, to let itself be studied by a sociologist interested in market reform.

2. The influence of the transformation on the way of thinking of sociologists is more subtle.[4] Dominant before 1980, in Polish sociology and in society, was the conviction that there was no serious or feasible alternative to the prevailing system. The system managed to create a narrow cognitive horizon, beyond which it was difficult to step. Within these bounds, it was assumed without reflection that the surrounding system had features of permanence and was not subject to the laws of time. After 1980 this "distortion" in the thinking of sociologists gave way to "thinking about a Poland which can be very different". It is for this reason that sociology was not fully unprepared intellectually for the coming of democracy.

3. Democratic change of the system in Poland is increasing the reliability of sociological studies, particularly survey research.

---

[4]See P. Lukasiewicz, Socjologia ograniczona, "Krytyka" 1991 no. 34-35.

There has been a reduction in the oppressiveness of that nightmare of two realms of opinion--official and private. Official opinions used to be supported by organs of authority and declared in public situations. Because an interview is a public situation, the people were inclined to declare official opinions, and to conceal private ones. The conformism with official standards has weakened, but has not been eliminated. The mere change of political institutions is not enough; a sense of breakthrough at the bottom is also needed, the disappearance of the division between "them" and "us". It is known that people change more slowly than institutions; in any case, these institutions are also changing more slowly than people would have expected.

The state monopoly on public language had already been broken by the 1980s. That monopoly had made it difficult for people to formulate opinions deviating from official ones, and at the same time made it hard for sociologists to grasp convictions deviating from those propagated from above. The monopoly of the authorities over public language was broken by the Church, Solidarity and the democratic opposition.

In association with the sudden development of public opinion research in recent years, it is increasingly rare for respondents to treat a sociological interview as an official situation, in particular as a way for authorities to check on what citizens think. This must have increased the reliability of survey answers. The process of acculturation to survey studies, because that is what is being discussed here, is far from complete. Partly as a result of habits shaped under the previous system and partly under the inducement of the model of "the good citizen", those surveyed in post-electoral polls show a steady tendency to declare their participation in an election, in spite of the fact that they did not vote.

4. Democracy in Poland has lifted political restrictions on freedom of speech, and therefore also on scientific publications. "Publications" in 99 copies, so characteristic of the previous period, have already disappeared. According to the law of that time, only such publications were free of censorship, and a very important part of the output of critical sociology in the 1980s--reports on research, case studies and syntheses--appeared in such a form. The circulation of the results of research and sociological idea has undergone a considerable improvement.

3. The new roles of sociologists

Social changes in Poland are creating a demand for sociologists in new roles which go beyond the activities of the social scientist or industrial sociologist which are traditional in this country.

1. The first role, or rather role-set, is the role of the social expert: political advisor, scientific interpreter and commentator on social phenomena. Operating in various state offices and political parties are teams of advisors which include sociologists, or use their services. Sociologists take part in the planning of election campaigns. The faces of sociologists frequently appear on the TV, and their texts appear frequently in newspapers. "Zycie Warszawy", one of the biggest dailies in this country, even runs a weekly sociological column.

Sociologists - as experts on society - supply several kinds of knowledge: simple, factual information about society; knowledge about a deeper structure of interest groups and values in a society; information about possible results of social undertakings and suggestions of practical solutions. Models of cooperation between experts and politicians are now being created. It is difficult to say what politicians think of their advisors. Sociologists, on the other hand, often express the opinion that politicians could do with their knowledge if for no other reason than that political elites overestimate the degree of interest and even understanding of society in their programs, and reformers of the economy have insufficient sociological imagination.

Let us hope that sociological publications will play some role in facilitating an understanding amongst people about what is happening around them. Quite large fractions of Polish society hardly know in which direction the world is heading. They don't perceive the abstract rules of the game ("invisible hand"!), don't see their role in the transformations taking place and have no sense of their meaning. The unclearness of the situation is one of the sources of fear, and fear is one of the sources of pessimism in its evaluation and in foreseeing the future. It is probable that such attitudes appear during every big transformations, but this does not diminish their significance.

Currently, sociologist-experts are connected mainly with institutions of power and focus their activities around them. Previously, from the end of the 1970s, they were connected with social movements like Solidarity and various other kinds of alternative movements. Both social movements, and the interest in them on the part of sociologists, have lost some of their significance today. Here is a meaningful illustration: The Social Movements Research Committee of the Polish Sociological Association has decided to suspend its activities because its members have become involved in other matters: politics, journalism, business--activities which have become possible thanks to the social movements which they studied previously.

2. In the last three years, an unprecedented development of research into public opinion and the market has taken place in Poland. This is understandable in a situation in which public opinion freed itself

and the market began to take shape. Side by side with large state public opinion research centres there are already at least twenty new private establishments, both large and small, competing for the market. Almost every day newspapers present the results of the latest surveys. Plainly, surveys have become fashionable, and the role of the pollster has become an attractive profession for sociologists. Some sociologists have given up their universities and institutes for this, others treat opinion research as a source of additional income, and work in centers for opinion and market research (preferably their own!) is valued amongst graduates of sociology. In the face of difficulties for sociologists in the job market, a lot of students gear themselves up for the job of pollster; in the Institute of Sociology of the University of Warsaw classes in the techniques of advertizing, marketing and opinion research are enjoying great success. This seems to be some sort of <u>signum temporis</u>.

Neither market research nor public opinion research is strictly sociological research but both are conducted with methods worked out by sociologists. They provide material for sociology and they are widely considered to be sociological. This last consideration contributes to the fact that sociology is a science perhaps more visible to society today than at any other time. On the other hand, however, sociologists do not always look favourably on this branch of research. In Poland, there is no institutional control of surveys (of the kind undertaken by the French Commission de Sondages or the German ADM - Arbeitskreis Deutscher Makrtforschungs-Institute), and since some centers conduct research of very low quality, sociologists are trying to gain some control of them for the sake of professional reputation.

3. Social problems in Poland are intensifying with the continuing economic difficulties and the breakdown of the patronage state. Besides unemployment, which is the most massive problem, there are, for example, problems of old people, drug addiction or "ordinary" misery. For this reason, a demand has arisen for specialists in social problems, and for social workers. However, it would seem that the trend of Polish sociology in this direction is still weak.

4. New methods of research

Changes as serious as those which have occurred in Polish sociology could not leave untouched the instrumentarium of Polish sociology. In this respect, the most important change took place a long time ago, around 1980. Generally speaking, this involved a break with the dominance of the questionnaire model, and a pluralization of the methodology of social research.[5]

The empirical sociology shaped in the late 1950s treated a society as an aggregate of individuals, it focused on social consciousness and neglected the historical dimension of social phenomena. No wonder, then, that the basic type of data for it were the statements of individuals, usually survey answers. Such a survey was commonly considered to be a truly scientific method, and other methods were considered as something fundamentally worse. In the 1970s, anti-positivist currents reached Poland. These put into question the theoretical basis of the questionnaire, if we assume that it ever had one, or brought their non-existence to light, if we assume that it did not. However, the changes in society itself were more important.

Surprise at the mass protests of 1980 prompted sociologists to reflect critically on their array of methods. Rapid social changes also embraced the rejection of old, and the emergence of new, categories of thinking. The survey is rather poorly suited, while quantitative methods considerably more suitable. Society began to act--and moreover act as a whole. This no longer required surveys, but rather participant observation of social movements, research into real behaviour, statistical research into large organizations and analyses of the biographies of leadership elites. Many small social movements and alternative groups came into being and, again, it was only possible to study them by living with them, analyzing the texts which they produced and conducting in-depth interviews with their members. Obviously, these changes did not lead to the abandonment of surveys, as other factors mitigated in their favour such as the development of public opinion research and the increase in the reliability of answers. But the formula "Sociological research - survey research" has disappeared, and the survey has ceased to be considered as the scientific method, but simply as one of the important tools used by sociologists.

This important breakthrough in the consciousness and methodological practice of sociologists has already taken place, but the changes of the last few years have ushered in new pressures. The advent of the market has activated the development of market research, and from it there has come the focused group interview, a method suited perfectly to the recognition of conceptual categories of social groups, of patterns of thinking, or of social perception. The limitation on funds for research has forced sociologists to stay away from large-scale (and expensive) surveys and to seek possibilities for cheaper non-questionnaire studies: statistical analyses, analyses of existing official

---

[5]See Sułek, TThe Rise and Decline of urvey Sociology" in Poland, <u>Social Research</u>, forthcoming.

materials, intensive interviewing of small social groups carefully selected with regard to their typicality or social significance, and case studies of institutions and local communities.

It can be said that, as society becomes more and more pluralistic, sociological methodology also becomes pluralistic.

5. Disadvantageous changes in sociology

All of the changes in sociology mentioned up to this point--the appearance of new areas of research, the increased freedom of scientific inquiry, the emergence of new roles within the sociological profession and the methodological diversification of social studies--are positive results of the systemic change in Poland. However, the transformation does not always influence sociology in an advantageous way.

1. The new possibilities for public activities which have opened up for people coming from circles opposed to real socialism drew many sociologists away from social science and into politics. Instead of interpreting the world they began to change it. It is quite telling that, at the time this article was being written in April 1992, the head of the President's Office and the Deputy Speaker of the Sejm were sociologists; and two ministers (from departments as diverse as National Defence and Culture) and three deputy ministers are also sociologists. It is to be hoped that the political activity of sociologists will turn out, in the long run, to be a scientifically-inspiring experience for them, and will enrich sociology. For the time being, however, distracting sociologists from interpreting the world makes this science the poorer.

2. Scientific work and academic life have been reduced in their attractiveness. In the period of real socialism, universities and the Polish Sociological Association were oases of political freedom and attractive because of their unique possibilities for independent thought. Today such possibilities exist everywhere, so many sociologists are transferring their energy to other areas - to politics, journalism and business. A scientific career has also lost some of its attraction as a result of the general pauperization of the intelligentsia and scientists. who are now paid from an increasingly limited state budget.

3. State expenditure on scientific research has been reduced and the principles for the financing of research have been changed. The financing of huge five-year projects, connected with consecutive five-year economic plans, has come to an end. A system of grants has been launched, distributed by a central government body (the Committee on Scientific Research) on the basis of competition between researchers applying for them. For sociologists, a time of uncertainty has begun. They must--more than at any other time--strive for research funding and

seek new sponsors, including those abroad. The general reduction in the expenditure of the state on scientific research does not allow the intellectual potential of sociology to be used fully for the study of the unique historical experience which the systematic transformation is, nor the processes of transformation as one of the factors in the success of that transformation. The lack of money in the state exchequer for social research even threatens the existence of some sociological institutions. This has induced Andrzej Rychard and Edmund Wnuk-Lipiński to the bitter remark that while sociology managed under Communism, there is no certainty that it will manage under democracy.[6]

4. The type of texts written by sociologists has changed. The phenomena which interest them are happening before their eyes, processes are rapid, and sociologists themselves have neither the temporal nor often the necessary emotional distance. Sociologists are therefore not always able to write in-depth analyses of the results of empirical studies, or dissertations meeting high academic standards. Instead of articles for professional journals, they often write essays for magazines aimed at a wider audience, or articles for daily or weekly newspapers.

5. In an important part of the sociological community, there has been a weakening of the strong sense of "togetherness" which marked the previous system. This has happened as a result of several circumstances: Along with the breakdown of the Communist rule, the sense of threat and being in opposition to a common enemy has vanished. In association with the appearance of political conflicts within the victorious camps of Solidarity and political parties, sociologists declared themselves to be on different sides and directed their sympathies towards different parties and politicians; one should add to this the sociologists faithful to the post-Communist party. Along with the reduction in government spending on science, and the emergence of a market for social research, sociologists have begun to compete for limited budget resources, grants and orders from the market. These changes are a fragment of the processes observed throughout society. It seems, however, that in spite of many disintegrating factors, the sense of togetherness in the sociological tribe is still considerable. It was long-lasting and so strong that it is weakening only slowly.

The negative and rather unexpected changes in the Polish sociology of the transformation period, that are enumerated here, are by no means something peculiar to Poland. Almost all items covered here

---

[6]A. Rychard, E. Wnuk-Lipiński, Sytuacja nauk społecznych-diagnoza i propozycje poprawy, 1991, unpiblished memorandum.

(1,3,4,5) have been outlined by Rudolf Andorka in his consideration of contemporary Hungarian sociology.[7]

6. A final remark

In this paper I have shown how the systemic change in Poland is causing numerous and beneficial changes in Polish sociology. It is generating new areas of research, increasing the freedom of science, creating new roles for sociologists and promoting methods for their research. I have also shown, however, that sociology is paying a certain price for the transformation, and not a trifling one: resources for social research have been reduced, sociologists are showing a tendency to give up research for the sake of other activities and to write popular articles instead of scientific dissertations. In the new conditions, the community of sociologists is no longer as cohesive as before. There can be no doubt that the democratic change of the system in Poland is, from the point of view of the interests of sociology as a science, an extremely happy event.

However, it is also obvious that negative results of the transformation limit its positive significance seriously. It remains for us merely to believe that the professionalism and adaptability of Polish sociology will allow it to cope with the difficulties of the transformation period and to utilize the opportunities which the transformation has opened up for it.

---

[7] R. Andorka, Hungarian Sociology in the Face of the Political, Economic and Social Transition, *International Sociology* 1991 Vol. 6 No. 4 pp. 465-469.

INDEX

r